Yorkshire Dales Teashop Walks

Jean Patefield

COUNTRYSIDE BOOKS
NEWBURY BERKSHIRE

First published 1997
© Jean Patefield 1997
Reprinted 2003, 2008

Revised and updated 2015

COUNTRYSIDE BOOKS
3 Catherine Road
Newbury Berkshire

ISBN 978 1 85306 489 0

To view our complete range of books,
please visit us at
www.countrysidebooks.co.uk

Designed by Graham Whiteman
Cover illustration by Colin Doggett
Photographs and maps by the author

Produced through The Letterworks Ltd., Reading
Typeset by KT Designs, St Helens
Printed by Berforts Information Press, Oxford

Contents

Wharfedale

The Western Dales

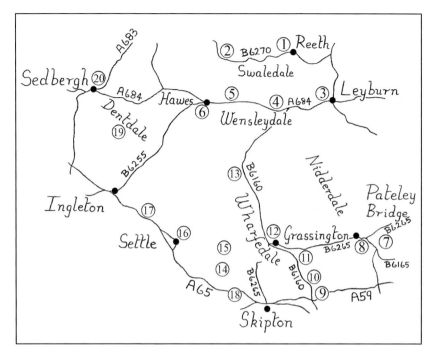

Area Map Showing Location of the Walks.

KEY TO SKETCH MAPS

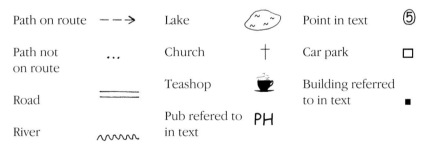

Path on route	— — →	Lake	Point in text ⑤
Path not on route	...	Church †	Car park ▢
Road	═══	Teashop ☕	Building referred to in text ■
River	∿∿∿	Pub refered to in text PH	

INTRODUCTION

'In all my travels I've never seen a countryside to equal in beauty the Yorkshire Dales. The Dales have never disappointed me.' So wrote the Bradford born author J. B. Priestley, and who can disagree with him? The importance of this landscape was recognised in 1954 when the Yorkshire Dales were designated a National Park. The National Park Authority now has planning control as well as providing information and ranger services and maintaining footpaths. But within the underlying unity of the National Park each dale has its own character, so the walks in each dale are presented together.

Swaledale is the most northerly of the major dales. It has an austere beauty and unity that distinguishes it from the others. The Norse influence is very strong here with strange sounding place names such as Muker, Keld and Arkengarthdale. Before the Norsemen the Romans came here to win the lead from the hills, an industry that continued well into the 19th century. The other particularly outstanding feature is the flower filled meadows, seen at their best in early summer. The wild remoteness of Swaledale means that teashops are to be found in only a few places and so only two walks are described here, but they are both highly recommended.

Wensleydale is the most pastoral of the major dales, broad and green with a long tradition of dairy farming and, of course, cheese making. The valley has two of everything: two market towns (Leyburn and Hawes), two important waterfalls (Aysgarth and Hardraw), two castles (Bolton and Middleham), two main side valleys (Bishopdale and Coverdale), two roads and two National Park information centres, at Aysgarth and Hawes. The exception to this doubling is the single Roman fort at Bainbridge. There is no uniformity about the settlements along the valley. Each town and village has its own, very distinctive character, perhaps reflecting the rugged individuality of this most Yorkshire of dales. The four walks described in these pages are similarly diverse.

When the Yorkshire Dales National Park was created in 1954, Nidderdale was excluded because most of the valley above Pateley Bridge is associated with providing water for Bradford. In the past, water authorities were determined to keep the public away from reservoirs and the catchment areas which feed them; but in recent decades there has been a general change in policy and the public are now welcomed. This has opened up Nidderdale far more to walkers and it has now been declared an Area of Outstanding Natural Beauty. Hence my decision to include it in this book. The two walks described are both different but have one feature in common – stunning views!

Five walks are described in Wharfedale. Rising high in the hills, the river Wharfe flows south-east for about 60 miles before merging with the Ouse and then on to the Humber. The lower part of the valley is excluded from the National Park and so has not been included in this book. Above all else, Wharfedale has magnificent scenery dominated by Great Scar limestone and in the upper dale white scars of rock etch the valley sides, sometimes to dramatic effect as at Kilnsey Crag. The great monasteries once controlled vast tracts of land here and in more recent centuries the area round Bolton Abbey has been owned by the Dukes of Devonshire so there is plenty of historic interest. Nowhere is the road more than a couple of miles from the river so Wharfedale is easily accessible. Thus the dale can be busy but that means there are plenty of teashops to sample.

In this last section I have included all the walks on the western side of the Dales. In the north, Dent and Sedbergh are no longer in the county of Yorkshire, having been transferred by local government reorganisation into the county of Cumbria, but they are in the National Park and therefore included in this book. Dent and Dentdale in particular have perhaps more a feel of the Lake District, without a lake, of course!

All the walks in this book are between 2½ and 6 miles long and should all be within the capacity of the average person, including those of mature years and families with children. They are intended to take the walker through this outstanding corner of England at a gentle pace with plenty of time to stop and stare, to savour the beauty and interest all around.

Certain of the walks involve some climbing. This is inevitable as hills add enormous interest to the countryside and with no hills there are no views. However, this presents no problem to the sensible walker who has three uphill gears – slowly, very slowly and admiring the view. None of the walks in this book are inherently hazardous but sensible care should be taken. Many of the falls which do happen are due to unsuitable footwear, particularly unridged soles since grass slopes can be as slippery as the more obviously hazardous wet, smooth rock. Proper walking shoes or boots also give some protection to the ankle. It is also essential to look where you are putting your feet to avoid tripping up. Wainwright, the doyen of walkers in the Lake District, said that he never had a serious fall in all his years and thousands of miles of walking because he always looked where he put his feet and stopped if he wanted to admire the scenery.

All the routes are on public rights of way or permissive paths and have been carefully checked but, of course, in the countryside things do change; a gate is replaced by a stile or a wood is extended. Each walk is circular and is illustrated by a sketch map, designed to guide you to the starting point and give a simple yet accurate idea of the route to be taken. However, an

Ordnance Survey map is useful as well, especially for identifying the main features of views. The Ordnance Survey produce three maps in their Outdoor Leisure series at 2½ inches to the mile, numbers 2, 19, and 30, which cover the area and are very useful. Nidderdale is covered by Explorer 298. The appropriate Outdoor Leisure or Explorer maps and the grid reference of the starting point are given for each walk.

The walks are designed so that, starting where suggested, the teashop is reached in the second half. Thus a really good appetite for tea can be worked up and then its effects walked off. Some walks start at a car park, which is ideal. Where this is not possible, the suggested starting place will always have somewhere a few cars can be left without endangering other traffic. However, it sometimes fits in better with the plans for the day to start and finish at the teashop and so for each walk there are details of how to do this.

Tea is often said to be the best meal to eat out in England and I believe that it is something to be enjoyed on all possible occasions. Scones with cream and strawberry jam, delicious home-made cakes, toasted teacakes dripping with butter in winter, delicate cucumber sandwiches in summer, all washed down with the cup that cheers and Yorkshire is known for its strong and sustaining tea! Bad for the figure maybe, but the walking will see to that.

The best teashops offer a range of cakes, all home-made and including fruit cake as well as scones and other temptations. Teapots should be capacious and pour properly. Most of the teashops visited on these walks fulfil all these criteria admirably and they all provide a good tea. They always serve at least light lunches as well so there is no need to think of these walks as just something for the afternoons.

The pleasures of summer walking are obvious. Many of the teashops featured in this book have an attractive garden where tea can be taken outside when the weather is suitable. However, let me urge you not to overlook the pleasures of a good walk in winter. The roads and paths are quieter and what could be better than sitting by an open fire in a cosy teashop scoffing crumpets that you can enjoy with a clear conscience due to the brisk walk to get them!

Teashops are not scattered evenly through the Dales. In some places popular with tourists, the visitor is spoilt for choice. In such cases the teashop that, in my opinion, most closely fulfils the criteria set out above is recommended but should that not appeal, there are others from which to choose. In other places where there is a delightful walk to be enjoyed, the choice for tea is more limited. However, they all offer a good tea part way round an attractive walk.

The opening times, telephone number and website where available of each teashop is given. Some are rather vague about when they open out of season – it seems to depend on weather and mood. If you are planning a walk on a wet November Tuesday, for example, a call to check that tea will actually be available that day is a wise precaution. A few are definitely closed in the depths of winter and for these walks an alternative source of refreshment is given. In most cases, these are pubs serving food which in some cases includes tea.

So put on your walking shoes and prepare to be delighted, by the scenery of the Yorkshire Dales and a traditional English tea!

Jean Patefield

Walk 1
HEALAUGH AND REETH

This walk is a cocktail of the best countryside Swaledale has to offer. The outward leg climbs up the side of the dale for some extensive views followed by a gentle and easy descent which is a delight to walk. After visiting the ancient and interesting settlement of Reeth, the return is an attractive stroll along the bank of the river Swale.

 Overton House Café is a modern take on the traditional teashop, with an attractive bright interior and some tables outside overlooking the extensive green in Reeth. The cakes include homemade shortbread and fruit cake with Wensleydale cheese. The lunch menu is displayed on a blackboard and changes regularly but includes a choice of sandwiches, snacks such as Yorkshire rarebit with bacon and chutney and full meals. The opening hours change with the seasons so check the website for up to date information. Telephone: 01748 884045. Website: www.overtonhousecafe.com

DISTANCE: 4 miles.
MAP: OL30 Yorkshire Dales Northern & Central Areas.
STARTING POINT: The layby on the B6270, ½ mile west of Healaugh (GR 012985).
HOW TO GET THERE: The B6270 is the main road through Swaledale.
ALTERNATIVE STARTING POINT: If you want to visit the teashop at the beginning
   or end of your walk, start in Reeth where there is ample parking around the green,
   overlooked by Overton House Café. You will then start the walk at point 9.

THE WALK

1. Return to the road and turn right. Just before entering Healaugh, turn left on a lane signed 'Kearton 1'.

Healaugh today is a quiet cluster of cottages overlooking the river below and moors above. Its population is much reduced from its heyday at the height of the lead mining boom last century – in 1851 its population was 251, including 112 children under 14. Earlier, in the 13th and 14th centuries, the area was famous for its wild boar and wolves – animals we need not fear today! John of Gaunt, who had a castle at Knaresborough near Harrogate, had a hunting lodge here.

2. Turn right up the drive to Thiernswood Hall, signed as a bridleway. Immediately before an imposing house, turn right.

3. When the track ends, turn right over a rather obscure stile immediately after an arched barn on the right and before some steps. Pass another arched barn on the left and go through a gateway. Head across a field to walk with a wall on the left, through a gated stile and then bear left across a track in front of a house to a gate in a wall. Turn right. Go through a small gate ahead and up by a wall on the left. Pass some tumbledown buildings to two gates.

4. Go through the gate on the left, and bear slightly left across a small field to again go through the left one of two gates. Carry on up by a wall on the right to a surfaced track. A few yards to the right, turn left on to an unsurfaced track to continue on more or less the same direction. At an oblique cross path, bear right to shortly walk with a wall on the right. When the path forks, bear left up to the corner of a wall and walk by the wall for a few yards to a squeeze stile.

5. Walk with a wall on the right to the far end of the field. Cross another

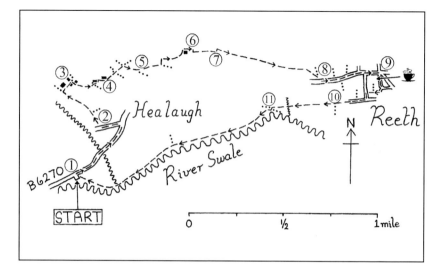

squeeze stile and then turn left through a gap in the wall. Head up the right-hand side of a field to another gap and then turn right to a gated squeeze stile. Continue in the same direction across a field to a gap in a wall. Now bear left to go to the left of a house. Go through a gate and bear right behind the house and ahead to a further gate.

6. Turn right and go through another gate then turn left and take a path between two walls.

As you walk the next part of the route, look across the valley where there are several interesting features to be seen. Looking at the fields, outlined by the ubiquitous dry stone walls, it is easy to see how the intake land was won from the moor. In one place, the shape of the fields resembles a milk jug. There are also traces of lead mines and a small Roman fort, probably built on the site of an earlier Iron Age settlement as the remains of hut circles have been discovered. A local story tells that the first tea drunk in England was at Swale Hall below the moor, just beyond Reeth. Apparently it was boiled up with milk and sugar and then drunk, leaves and all!

7. Shortly after the wall on the right ends, go through a squeeze stile on the left and diagonally right to a small gate. Thankfully, the path is now much more straightforward. It is not readily apparent on the ground at the time of writing but is easy to follow across the fields from stile to stile, all the time heading gently downwards towards a road. Not far from the road, in a field with prominent terraces, the stile has been shifted left uphill from its proper line. You will find it where a stretch of fence and a wall join. In the next field head down to the far right-hand corner and the road.

In the next to last field note the lynchets or strip terraces. These are found in many places (see walk 17 for another example) and were laid out by farmers in the Middle Ages to avoid the soil erosion that would otherwise result from cultivating crops on a hillside. Barley, oats. peas, beans and rye were grown.

8. Turn left and walk down into Reeth. At the Buck Hotel turn right and the teashop is on the right.

One glance at Reeth indicates how important it has been in the past with fine three-storey buildings overlooking a spacious green. The view from the green looking down the valley towards Grinton is magnificent. Standing at the junction of Swaledale and Arkengarthdale, Reeth is the natural site for a market and the town was granted its charter in 1695, holding seven fairs a year as well as a weekly market, still held today on a Friday. The fairs declined with the collapse of local lead mining (see walk 2). Of greater interest to present-day visitors are the craft shops supported by the main business of today – tourism. There is also the excellent Swaledale Folk Museum with displays on the dale's main industries down the years – farming and lead mining. It is housed in the old Methodist Sunday School, tucked away behind the post office and is open every day between Easter and the end of October (telephone: 01748 884373).

9. After tea continue along the right-hand side of the green and take the lane out at the far end. Bear right along a walled alley. Turn left at a T-junction with a road and then right along a lane signed 'Swing Bridge'. Continue along this until you reach two gates across it.

10. Go through the one on the right along a path signed 'Healaugh'. Stay on this path until it approaches the river then take a path down a small, steep valley to the river bank.

11. Walk upriver, back to the start.

Walk 2
MUKER AND THWAITE

This route explores the popular area of Swaledale round Kisdon Fell. It is essentially a valley walk, the circuit leading up one valley and down the next. The two are connected by a path over the shoulder of Kisdon Fell so there is a little climbing involved. The most notable feature, apart from the attractive views, is the enormous number of squeeze stiles encountered. These are sometimes called 'fat man's agony' but as they are quite capacious, there is no need for a girth warning on this walk!

The only problem you are likely to encounter on this route is having to choose where to take tea. Kearton Country Hotel in Thwaite is well positioned in the last third of the walk, just when a cup of tea is most welcome. It serves cream teas, excellent Danish pastries, toasted teacakes and muffins. Hot food is available between noon and 5 pm. It has a few tables outside and is open every day. Telephone: 01748 886277. Website: www.keartoncountryhotel.co.uk

If you want to visit a teashop before or after your walk, I suggest Muker Teashop. It is attached to the village shop and has open fires indoors and some tables outside. In the summer it is open every day, except Tuesday, from 10.30 am to 5 pm, and weekends in the winter. There are some interesting suggestions on the menu such as Old Peculier fruit cake with Swaledale cheese or Yorkshire rarebit with home-cooked ham. Telephone: 01748 886409. Website: www.mukervillage.co.uk

DISTANCE: 6 miles.

MAP: OL30 Yorkshire Dales Northern & Central Areas.

STARTING POINT: The public car park at Muker (GR 911977), for which there is a charge. If this is full, there is space to leave cars by the road at the west end of the village.

HOW TO GET THERE: Muker is on the B6270 Reeth to Nateby road.

THE WALK

1. From the car park turn left over the bridge. Take the first road on the right. Pass the church and village hall then bear left round a house called Armsleigh. Turn left along a lane signed 'Public Footpath to Keld'. This soon becomes a roughly surfaced track and climbs gently to give superb views of Swaledale.

Muker is an ancient place whose odd name (pronounced Mewker) derives from the Norse Meukahew meaning a small cultivated farm. An attractive huddle of cottages around a church, chapel and village Institute, it has been a farming community for most of its long history. For a brief period between the 17th and mid-19th centuries lead mining flourished in Upper Swaledale and swelled the population. Richard and Cherry Kearton, pioneer nature photographers from the neighbouring village of Thwaite, were educated here and the building which was once the school, now a teashop, has a plaque to them.

2. When the track bends sharp left, leave it to continue in the same direction through a metal field gate on an enclosed path.

3. As the path approaches the river at a barn, bear left to follow a path upriver along the top of a bank. This soon reaches the river bank where there are many delightful spots to linger.

4. After about ¾ mile, watch for a somewhat dilapidated wall coming down towards the river. Cross this at a squeeze stile indicated by a yellow marker. (Do not continue on the path on the river bank.) Follow this path

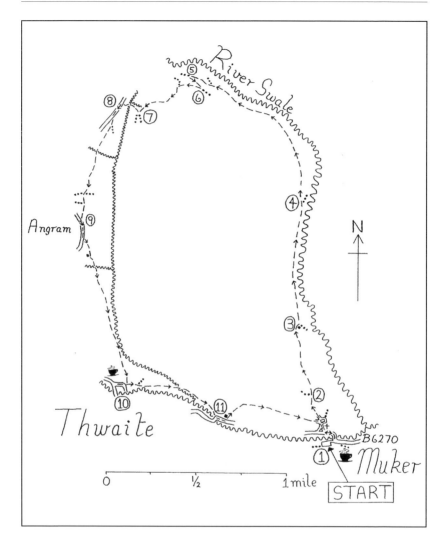

across fields from stile to stile, eventually rising above the river. After several fields (nine to be precise) the path is enclosed between tumbledown walls and then enters a wood.

It is hard to imagine this lovely valley was once an important centre of lead mining but time and nature have healed the scars. If you look carefully, you will be able to see evidence of the former industry. Lead was exported from Swaledale from Roman times onwards and it is said to have been used to seal the roofs of both the

Tower of London and St Peter's in Rome. In the middle of the last century well over 1,000 people were employed directly in mining as well as all the ancillary trades such as carters and blacksmiths. The industry collapsed in the last quarter of the 19th century, made uneconomic by cheaper foreign imports. Many of the miners moved away to find work in coal mines, never to return.

5. After further ¼ mile, some 30 yards after the path starts to descend, take a clear path on the left, marked by a tumbledown cairn and signed 'Pennine Way FP Thwaite Muker'.

6. Immediately after passing through a gap in a wall, turn right on a fainter path. This initially follows the wall on your right but soon veers left and becomes faint. Walk on round the hill to meet a cross-wall near a sheep pen (a small walled enclosure) by a gate. Turn left to walk with this wall on your right. Turn right through a gate onto a clear path with a wall on the right. Follow this to a cross track.

The route is now passing over the shoulder of Kisdon, a small hill which is separated from the main mass. This unusual feature arose after the Ice Age. Before this, Kisdon was part of Gunnerside Moor and the Swale flowed down a more westerly valley the route soon follows. However, the valley became blocked by glacial debris, forcing the water of the melting glaciers to find a new path. It broke through into a small valley to the east, the present course of the Swale, before rejoining the original valley at Muker. A smaller beck, Skeb Skeugh, now flows round the western flank of Kisdon which was once the course of the Swale.

7. Turn right to a road.

This track is part of the Corpse Road. Until the middle of the 16th century, when the chapel was built at Muker, the only consecrated ground in the whole of Upper Swaledale was at Grinton. The parish extended as far as the Westmorland border and corpses had to be taken to the Cathedral of the Dales at Grinton to be buried. The bodies were transported in light wicker coffins drawn on sledges or carried on the shoulders of relatives. When the church was built at Muker in 1580 the journey was shortened, though still considerable. The Queen's Head Inn in Muker (no longer a pub) kept special funeral mugs hanging in the kitchen for bearers who were thirsty after carrying their burden from Keld and farms even further up the dale.

8. Turn left for 120 yards then turn left again through a small wooden gate signed 'Angram ½ML'. Bear half right to a gap in a wall. Now bear right to a small gate. The path from here is not readily apparent on the ground but is easy to navigate between gates and stiles, always going in roughly the same direction, until you reach the road again.

This hamlet is Angram. It is the highest village in the Dales, being 1,185 feet above sea level. The Vikings are often depicted as wild men in horned helmets, raping and pillaging their way round the countryside. Less often they are shown doing what they did most, settling on the land for a peaceful and productive life of farming. Their influence was strong in the Dales and most of the somewhat unusual village names found hereabouts are of Norse origin.

One feature of this walk, apart from the enormous number of stiles, is the barns, one of which is found in nearly every field. The main reason for this is the system of inheritance, unusual for England, found in this part of the world. Known as gavelkind, the parents' estate was divided up between all the children, eventually resulting in tiny holdings, perhaps just a single field. Employment in lead mining was supplemented with stock keeping, hence the need for a barn in most fields. In this century the farms have been amalgamated into viable holdings and some barns are now redundant and falling into disrepair.

☕ **9.** Turn left for 230 yards then take a public footpath on the left, heading half right downhill to the left of the ubiquitous barn. Continue on, across the fields towards Thwaite, now seen ahead, and again navigating from stile to stile on a more clearly defined path. Follow this round to the left of some barns to the road in Thwaite. Turn right to the teashop.

Thwaite is well known to those hardy souls who walk the Pennine Way and descend here from their labours on Great Shunner Fell. The Kearton brothers were born here. They were pioneers in photographing nature with both still and movie cameras and were skilled in making hides, once even mounting a camera inside a stuffed cow! Richard was born in 1862 and was crippled as a result of a childhood accident. A London publisher, staying locally for a shoot, was impressed by the young man's knowledge and enthusiasm for natural history and offered him a job. Before long Richard was writing his own books, illustrated by his and Cherry's photographs. He was able to retire in 1898 on the income from his books and became a friend of the American President Teddy Roosevelt. His younger brother, Cherry, was born in 1871 and was perhaps the more famous through both his films and radio broadcasts. He was killed by a German bomb which fell outside Broadcasting House in 1940.

10. Retrace your steps and take the path signed 'Pennine Way Keld 3ml Muker 1ml'. Keep ahead, ignoring the path to your left by which you arrived.

Continue ahead when the Pennine Way shortly branches off left and follow the clear path, again walking from stile to stile and crossing a stream at a bridge.

11. At a road turn left. After 150 yards turn left along the drive to some cottages, signed 'Muker'. Turn right through the first gate and after passing through a second gate head diagonally left across a field to a gate near the top right-hand corner. Through the gate continue on the clear path by a wall and follow this through yet more squeeze stiles. In Muker follow the lane into the village and then retrace your steps to the start.

Walk 3
WENSLEY AND LEYBURN

The highlight of this walk is the 1½ mile long section on Leyburn Shawl. This is a limestone scar with an easy path along the top, laid out in the 19th century. Visitors flocked to admire the famous views, which are just as tremendous today. The path leads almost to the centre of Leyburn for tea after which a gentle stroll across the fields returns you to Wensley.

This walk offers the choice of two contrasting tea shops. Yorkshire Tea Party is a rural tea garden about a third of the way round the route which, at the time of writing, has no indoor accomodation and is only open in summer, 10 am to 5 pm most days. They are, however, hoping to have some indoor tables and extend the opening hours. Their speciality is scones, both delicious savoury scones and sweet ones served with clotted cream. There is also a selection of cakes and snacks to enjoy in the pretty garden. Telephone: 01969 624953, Website: www.yorkshireteaparty.co.uk

Leyburn, two-thirds of the way round, is popular with locals and visitors. The Posthorn, overlooking the Market Square has an appetising selection of cakes, temptingly displayed on a sideboard, such as Old Peculier fruit loaf with Wensleydale cheese. For lunch there are full meals, including a daily special and all day breakfast, as well as the usual snacks. It stocks a wide range of speciality teas and is open throughout the year from 9 am until 5 pm in summer and 10 am to 4 pm in winter. Telephone: 01969 622243.

DISTANCE: 5 miles.
MAP: OL30 Yorkshire Dales Northern & Central Areas.
STARTING POINT: Wensley church (GR 092895).
HOW TO GET THERE: Wensley is on the A684 Leyburn-Hawes road, 1½ miles or so west of Leyburn. There are some places to park without causing inconvenience by the church or, if that is not possible, by the bridge over the river Ure just south of the village.
ALTERNATIVE STARTING POINT: If you want to visit the teashop at the beginning or end of your walk, start in Leyburn where there is ample parking in the square or, on market day, in one of the car parks. The teashop is in the Market Square. You will then start the walk at point 9.

THE WALK
1. With your back to the church, turn right along the A684 and then left by the old pump on the green along the drive to Bolton Hall.

Today the trim settlement of Wensley is the estate village of Bolton Hall, seat of the Dukes of Bolton. It gives no hint of its former glories when it was the main market of the area, giving its name to the entire dale. The Black Death struck the community particularly viciously in 1563, a disaster from which it never recovered. Many of the survivors fled the town; the stricken were not buried in the churchyard but in a nearby field called Chapel Hill. Following this tragedy, Askrigg and Leyburn grew up to take its place as the main markets of the dale. The church dates from 1245, on the site of an earlier building. The Bolton pews look rather like theatre boxes. The story goes that they were built by the third Duke to please his wife who as Lavinia Fenton had played Polly Peachum in the first production of 'The Beggar's Opera'.

2. After passing a house on the right, turn off the drive through a field gate on the right. Head half left across a large field towards a small stone building, seen ahead.

3. On reaching this, walk with a fence on the left to a gate at the end of the

21

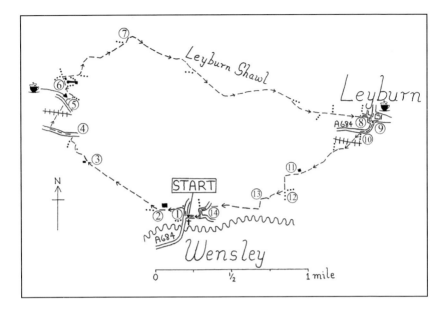

field. Head slightly left in the next field to a wooden field gate into a wood. When the path joins a track, turn right to a lane.

4. Turn left for 225 yards then take a public footpath on the right. Head diagonally right across a field to a gate over the railway line and then continue across a second field to a lane.

☕ **5.** Follow the track opposite, passing the tea garden, and continue on the main track round to the left when it forks.

6. The track reaches a farm. Just after the last farm building on the right, turn right along a track and follow this uphill to a gateway. Bear left on a clear track. When this fades out, bear round to the right to a stile by a field gate. Over the stile the path bears half left up to the left-hand corner of a wood.

7. Now turn right and follow this easy and delightful path for 1½ miles to Leyburn, staying always on the path along the top of the wood.

This is Leyburn Shawl, a great favourite with Victorian visitors to Leyburn for its easy walking and magnificent views. Tea Galas with music and dancing were organised here by a temperance organisation, The Band of Hope. In 1844 the Wensleydale Advertiser records that 2,000 people attended, 'the bulk of whom were of the highest respectability'. The path traverses the top of a scar of main limestone some 75 feet thick and sadly passes a working quarry at one point. The magnificent views in the other direction compensate for this, however.

Mary, Queen of Scots, was imprisoned at Bolton Castle, a few miles west. It is said that she once escaped and made it as far as here before being recaptured. In fact, she wasn't kept in close confinement and often went out on hunting expeditions and it is quite possible that she came as far as this.

8. The path emerges at the top of a lane. Turn right and then left at the main road and first right. The teashop is a few yards ahead on the left.

Though mentioned in the Domesday Book, Leyburn was a small village until the disastrous epidemic at Wensley gave the town its chance. It received a further boost with the coming of the railway in 1856. Today it is the main centre for Lower Wensleydale with an important livestock mart, a weekly market on Fridays and a variety of shops.

9. After tea leave the square along the A684 past the Bolton Arms.

10. Just after the last house on the left, as a track starts on the left, go through a field gate and head diagonally down across two fields and over the railway. The path now crosses the fields, heading in the direction of the flat-topped eminence of Pen Hill. It is not always readily apparent on the ground but easy to follow from stile to stile.

11. Soon after passing some barns on the right, crossing a stile brings you into a narrow field with no way through the substantial wall on the other side. At this point turn left.

12. At the top of a slight rise, as the river Ure below comes into view, cross a stile in the right-hand fence and continue in the same direction across a field and then along the right-hand side of the next. At the far end cross a stile on the right and continue in the same direction to the end of the field as Wensley comes into view.

13. After crossing the stile turn left and walk round the left-hand perimeter of a field. Follow the path across two more fields to emerge on a lane.

14. Turn left. At a T-junction turn right, back to Wensley church and the start.

Walk 4
AYSGARTH AND THE FALLS

If you enjoy riverside walking, this one should be on your 'must do' list! Much of the route is along the main river of Wensleydale, the Ure, near Aysgarth and it includes the deservedly famous falls. It also crosses over into the side valley of Bishopdale to enjoy a mile by Bishopdale Beck. This is a delightful walk with some excellent views as you descend into Bishopdale and is strongly recommended.

 Mill Race Teashop is in an 18th-century building and is particularly attractive with exposed beams and pine furniture. It offers a wide range of delicious cakes, including Black Sheep ale and chocolate cake. The giant homemade scones, of which there are usually several varieties, go down well plain, or served with lashings of jam and fresh cream. For lunch the menu includes a variety of platters, all are served with homemade breads and pickles or Yorkshire rarebit made with Wensleydale cheese and Black Sheep ale. From Easter throughout the summer it is open between

10.30 am and 5.30 pm. and in winter from 11 am until dusk at weekends and during the school holidays. Telephone: 01969 663446. Website: www.themillraceteashop.co.uk

When the teashop is closed, alternative sources of refreshment include the George and Dragon and Yoredale House, both in Aysgarth.

DISTANCE: 5 miles.

MAP: OL30 Yorkshire Dales Northern & Central Areas.

STARTING POINT: On the A684, ½ mile west of Aysgarth, at a footbridge over the river Ure where there are large parking areas on both sides of the bridge (GR 995888).

HOW TO GET THERE: The A684 is the main road through Wensleydale.

ALTERNATIVE STARTING POINT: If you want to visit the teashop at the beginning or end of your walk, start at the National Park car park at Aysgarth Falls (charge) from where there is a path down to the falls. The teashop is just over the bridge, on the left. You will then start the walk at point 12.

THE WALK

1. Return to the road and turn left for 350 yards.

2. Bear left on a path, unsigned at the time of writing, to a stile and the riverbank then bear right up to a higher level path which leads to a ladder stile into a field. (The lower path soon becomes very rough and can be under water when the river is in spate.) In the field pass to the right of a barn to a squeeze stile giving onto a track.

3. Turn left, soon passing the first of the waterfalls we shall enjoy today. This is not one of the famous ones – it is above High Force so perhaps should be called Ultra High Force.

4. At some buildings turn right on a signed path and follow this up across the fields to Aysgarth, seen above. The path is not readily apparent on the ground but is easy to follow from stile to stile and is indicated by yellow signs.

5. On reaching Aysgarth, go ahead to the main road and turn left. Take the first road on the right, signed 'Thoralby'.

An ancient village, mentioned in the Domesday Book, the name Aysgarth originally meant 'clearing in the oaks'. It is laid out on a Norman pattern with the church, passed later in the walk, some distance from the centre of the village. Despite its antiquity, the buildings today are relatively modern, being mainly 19th century.

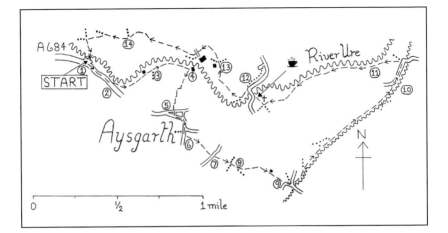

6. Just after the last house on the right, take a public footpath on the left signed 'Dykes House Lane ¼ML'. The path goes left across a field to a squeeze stile then bears right in the next field and straight across a third field to a lane.

7. Turn left and after 25 yards turn right on a public footpath signed 'Eshington Bridge ½ML'. Bear left to a stile near the far left corner of the field and then continue down a picturesque small valley and ahead at a signed cross path.

8. Watch for a stile in the wall on the left. Cross this, then continue in roughly the same direction, bearing to the left of some trees. Head leftwards down a field to a gap in a wall then turn right to walk with the wall on the right to a gate to the right of a barn. Now head steeply downhill to a lane seen below, crossing two stiles.

This path brings you into Bishopdale. As you walk down, notice the broad U shape of the valley. This was formed by the erosive force of the glacier which filled the valley in the Ice Age. When the ice melted the valley was filled with a lake and the silt deposited has given it a fertile floor. In the Middle Ages Bishopdale was part of the Honour of Middleham and reserved as a hunting chase. Farming only started in the 17th century when Middleham's ownership ended.

9. Turn left. At a road junction cross the road and take a path along the river bank, signed 'Hestholme Bridge ¾'. Continue on this path until it emerges at a road.

Notice the mounds in the field just before the road. These are moraines, or heaps of debris, eroded by a glacier and dropped here.

10. Turn right. Just before a bridge, at a track to Hestholme Farm, take a path on the left and follow it diagonally across a field to the bank of the river Ure.

The high ground bordering the river is a terminal moraine left as the glaciers retreated at the end of the Ice Age and it once impounded a huge lake in Wensleydale. Eventually, the river Ure broke through and eroded down to the bedrock. The rock here is alternating layers of resistant limestone and softer shale. The water has eroded into the shale and eventually the limestone has broken off, forming a series of attractive step-like falls. If you look carefully at the limestone you may be able to find fossils including those of brachiopods. These are small shelled creatures, commonly known as lamp shells, which at first glance resemble molluscs such as mussels. They were an important part of the fauna of the oceans millions of years ago when these rocks were laid down but the overwhelming majority of species are now extinct.

☕ **11.** Follow the path upstream, passing the Lower Force then climbing up above the river with glimpses of the spectacular Middle Force. Then bear slightly left to enter a wood at its left-hand corner. Follow the path through the wood, across a field and beside a church. Turn right immediately after passing the church and go down some steps at the far side of the churchyard to emerge on a lane at Yore Mill. The teashop is a few yards ahead, on the right.

St Andrew's is the parish church of Aysgarth. The size of the building and churchyard point to its former importance as the mother church for the whole of Upper Wensleydale. The present building is mainly 19th century but it contains an impressive wooden screen which dominates the south side of the chancel. It was brought here from Jervaulx Abbey after the Dissolution.

Yore Mill has had a chequered history. It was built as a cotton mill in 1784 then switched to corn and wool. A long mill race brought water from above the High Force to power a water wheel. Burned down in 1853, it was rebuilt twice as big. It is said to have produced the cloth for the red shirts worn by Garibaldi's revolutionary army in Italy. The water wheel was removed in 1937 and milling finished in 1959. After a period as a store for animal feed, it was converted into a Carriage Museum with exhibits including some 60 horsedrawn vehicles from the grand to the everyday as well as maps and other related items. It is open every day except over the Christmas period (telephone: 01969 663399).

12. After tea, continue over the bridge, from which there is an excellent view of the High Force. Immediately over the bridge take a path on the left, signed 'Askrigg 4m'. This soon leads to a picnic area by the river for which there is a small charge. Continue on the signed path, soon crossing a disused railway line.

The railway into Wensleydale from Leyburn to Askrigg was opened in 1877 and continued to Hawes in 1878. It was an important factor in opening up the dale to visitors, but it closed in April 1954.

13. The path now heads to the right of and then round behind a farm to a lane. Cross the lane and follow the path opposite, now walking beside the disused railway line. At the end of the second field, turn right alongside a wall to a stile and then turn immediately left.

14. As the starting point comes into view ahead and left, the path finally joins the line of the railway. Immediately before a footbridge over a farm track go down some steps on the left and then bear right across a field (beware bog!). At the end of the field cross a stile and turn left on a surfaced path, over a footbridge across the river, back to the start.

Walk 5
ASKRIGG AND BAINBRIDGE

All the walks in this volume are highly recommended but this one, above all others, encapsulates the essence of Wensleydale with a taste of everything that makes walking in this lovely dale such a joy. It visits two Dales villages, Bainbridge and Askrigg, each of which has its own teashop – two in Askrigg, so you won't go short of refreshment. Both villages are attractive and exceptionally interesting and, though only a few miles apart, they are very different in character. The route includes a stretch along a wooded limestone scar passing the site of a Roman fort, a visit to a spectacular waterfall and finishes with a short walk by the river Ure. If you can only spare the time for one expedition, this is the route I would suggest to best give you the flavour of the Yorkshire Dales in general, and Wensleydale in particular.

It is worth trying to time this walk to visit Askrigg Village Kitchen at lunch time to sample their delicious soups, which can be enjoyed with rolls and Wensleydale cheese. They also serve cheesy melts with interesting fillings such as black pudding with goats' cheese. Cakes include fruit cake served the Yorkshire way with cheese and they offer proper cream teas with clotted cream. Askrigg Village Kitchen is open every day throughout the year (except over the Christmas holiday) from 8 am to 4.30 pm, closing a little earlier in winter, and on Sunday afternoons in winter. Telephone: 01969 650076. Website:www.asktiggvillagekitchen.co.uk.

Also worthy of mention in Askrigg is Sykes House, opposite the church, which serves soup, sandwiches, and cakes until 5 pm Monday to Saturday and 2 pm on Sunday throughout the year. It was formerly a Temperance Hotel, note the large winged wheel sign on the wall. This is the emblem of the Cycle Touring Club and Sykes House has been a recommended stopping point for over 70 years. Telephone 01969 650535. Website: www.sykeshouse.co.uk.

The Corn Mill Tearoom in Bainbridge is an alternative choice in spring, summer and autumn. As you would guess. it is housed in a converted mill building and has a cheerful and bright interior with pine tables. They serve cakes, cream teas and a wide choice of ice creams. The walker's special, consisting of soup and a sandwich, is a good choice for lunch. They also serve Welsh rarebit and other things on toast and filled jacket potatoes, as well as breakfast until noon. The Corn Mill is open every day between 9.30 am and 5 pm from mid-March until the end of October. Telephone 01969 650212. Website: james-peacock.co.uk/

DISTANCE: 4½ miles.

MAP: OL30 Yorkshire Dales Northern & Central areas.

STARTING POINT: Worton Bridge near the village of Worton, where there is an informal parking space. (GR 955902)

HOW TO GET THERE: From the A684 Aysgarth Bainbridge road a mile east of Bainbridge take an unsigned lane north through the village to a bridge over the river Ure, to the parking just over the bridge.

ALTERNATIVE STARTING POINT: As well as three teashops, this walk has three possible starting points to fit in with the plans for the day. In addition to starting at Worton, it is possible to start in Askrigg, where there is some parking by the church. The teashop is across the road from the church. You will then start the walk at point 11. Alternatively, start in Bainbridge, where there is parking round the village green and pick up the route at point 6

THE WALK

1. Walk back over Worton bridge and through the village to the main road.

The tiny village of Worton was the scene of angry disturbances in 1757 when corn was delivered to the village for the upper dale and a riotous mob stole most of it, going on to demand money from the residents of Bainbridge and Askrigg. The leaders ended up in Richmond gaol.

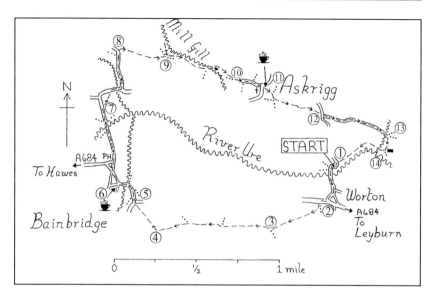

2. Turn right for 50 yards to a track on the left. Do not go along the track but immediately turn right off it along a path signed 'Bainbridge 2¼'. For some reason, the distance on this sign is given in kilometres rather than the usual miles. The path starts along the left-hand side of a field, round a hillock and then heads diagonally right towards trees, passing a sign at a fence corner. Continue in the same direction, passing the end of a broken wall, to a stile. This will be found just to the left of a kink in the wall ahead, at the bottom of the scar. Over the stile, bear right following the path up onto the scar.

3. Turn right along the scar, ignoring paths heading off the scar to the right.

Towards the end of the scar, look down to the right onto Brough Hill. This is the site of a Roman fort called Virosidium, connected by a road to the important military centre at Ribchester in Lancashire. It seems to have been an important outpost staffed by 500 soldiers to subdue the revolting natives and frequently attacked by the local Brigantes.

4. As Bainbridge comes into view the path bears right off the scar. It heads towards the village on a path going from stile to stile across fields to emerge at a road junction.

5. Turn left into Bainbridge along the A684, crossing the bridge over the river Bain with attractive falls to the left.

31

The river Bain is said to be the shortest river with its own name in England. It drains out of Semer Water and follows a steep two-mile course before flowing round the eastern edge of the village and into the Ure.

6. Bear right across the green and pass to the right of the Rose and Crown, a 500 year-old pub. Continue along the lane out of the village, ignoring a path to the right just after a bridge over the river.

Bainbridge is centred round a vast green, bought from the City of London in 1663 and managed by locally elected Lords Trustees. Dominating one end is the Rose and Crown, dating back to 1443, though it was much altered when the turnpike road was built in the 18th century. It houses the Bainbridge Horn, which was blown every night at 9 pm between Holy Rood (27 September) and Shrove Tuesday to guide in travellers. The custom originated in the days when Bainbridge was on the edge of a hunting forest, a wild and dangerous place. The horn is still occasionally blown.

7. Just before a road junction, go through a stile on the right and bear left across a field to rejoin the road. Turn right and take the first lane on the left.

This road junction is at the site of a Cistercian monastery established in 1145 by a group of monks led by Peter de Quincy from Savigny in Brittany. Despite their austere life and hard work, they did not flourish: they suffered a succession of bad crops and were troubled by wolves. Some monks left and the community then moved to Jervaulx and built their famous Abbey, the remains of which can still be seen. When the Wensleydale railway line was built it went through the burial ground revealing the bones of the unfortunates who perished here.

8. After about ¼ mile turn right along a track signed 'Mill Gill 500 YDS'. At the end of the second field bear left to a gated squeeze stile into a wooded ravine.

9. Over the stile, turn right along the top of the ravine. However, first take the path left and down into the ravine for a good view of Mill Gill Force and then retrace your steps. Follow the clear path along the top of the ravine, which eventually leads down to a footbridge over the river. Continue on the clear path behind some buildings and on across a field to a track.

The waterfall has formed due to the relative hardness of the various underlying rocks. At the top is a layer of limestone over a stratum of sandstone, which can also be seen on the west side as a vertical outcrop. At the bottom is shale, which is softer than the rocks above so it is worn away more quickly. This means the support of the rocks above is eroded away so they collapse. In this way the waterfall eats back forming, over thousands of years, the ravine we see today. This is thickly wooded with beech, sycamore and ash with a ground cover of typical woodland plants such as dog's mercury, bluebells, wild garlic and wood anemones. The buildings were once mills with machinery driven by water. Later they housed water driven generators which began providing power in 1908 making Askrigg one of the first villages round here to have electricity.

☕ **10.** Turn left along the track into Askrigg. At the church turn left to the teashop on the right.

Mentioned in the Domesday Book as Ascric, Askrigg had an important market before being granted a market charter in 1587 by Queen Elizabeth I. The market cross by the church is still to be seen. Set into the cobbles nearby is a ring to which bulls were tethered to be baited. Apart from the 'sport', such torment was thought to tenderise the meat. Small as it is by modern standards, Askrigg indubitably has the feel of a town with tall, tightly packed houses facing each other across the street as it winds its way up the hill.

The horse fair at Askrigg was famous and traders came from far and wide. Apparently, a farmer and his son murdered one Scottish trader as he was setting out for Swaledale on his way home. A courting couple behind a wall saw the whole dastardly deed and were bribed not to tell. The body was buried on the moor and the horse driven across the moor. Suspicion rested on the farmer and his son, suddenly flush with money, but nothing could be proven. The couple that had accepted the bribe did not prosper. Years later a buried body wrapped in a perfectly preserved plaid was found on the moor and buried at Grinton.

11. Take a track opposite the cross, Silver Street, signed 'Worton ¾ Aysgarth 4½'. Bear right at a T-junction. This soon becomes a walled path, which ends at an unusually well constructed squeeze stile giving into a field. Continue in the same direction along the left hand side of two fields and across a third to a lane.

12. Walk along a lane almost opposite for about ⅓ of a mile.

13. At a ford by an attractive old bridge, turn right along a track and bear to the right of farm buildings to a stile into a field.

14. Head across the field to a footbridge over a stream and on to a field gate into the next field. Walk upstream by the River Ure back to the start.

Walk 6
HAWES

As the centre of Upper Wensleydale, Hawes is a lively place, busy with both visitors and local people. The route described here soon leaves this bustle behind but not before passing one of the main industries of the town. Wensleydale Creamery makes wonderful cheese in the traditional manner. It welcomes visitors to see the cheese being made, learn something of its history, to taste and maybe to buy. The route then heads out into Sleddale where, on a clear day, there is a wonderful sense of the grandeur of the Dales. We return to Hawes for tea by Gayle Beck and Aysgill Force where there are many delightful spots to linger.

The Bay Tree in Hawes is a traditional Yorkshire teashop on the main street through Hawes and has some tables outside to watch the world go by in this bustling community. Hot and cold baguettes include the 'poor boy baguette' filled with ham, gruyere cheese, egg and salad and I am not sure why it should be for poor boys! For the seriously hungry there are daily specials such as steak pie. For tea there are delicious cakes set out on the sideboard. The unusual and delicious cream teas feature lemon scones served with lemon curd. They are open between 10 am and 4 pm every day throughout the year and close later in the summer. Telephone: 01969 667999.

DISTANCE: 3½ miles.

MAP: OL30 Yorkshire Dales Northern & Central areas or OL2 Yorkshire Dales Southern & Western areas.

STARTING POINT: The walk starts at a public car park (charge) at the west end of Hawes, 100 yards along a road signed 'Gayle ½ Kettlewell 15' and 'Wensleydale Cheese Visitor Centre' (GR 870898).

HOW TO GET THERE: Hawes is on the A684, the main road through Wensleydale.

ALTERNATIVE STARTING POINT: If you want to visit the teashop before your walk, start in the car park described. To get to the Bay Tree return to the main road and turn right. The teashop is in the middle of Hawes on the left. You will then start the walk at point 11. Alternatively, visit The Coffee Shop at the Creamery, passed at the end of point 1, which serves food that showcases their products.

THE WALK

1. Take a path on the right towards the rear of the car park and follow it across a field to the road, just by the Creamery.

Hawes is the home of Wensleydale cheese. Cheese making is an age-old method of preserving milk which may have been introduced to the Dales by monks. In the past, most Dales farms produced their own cheese. Large scale production started in Hawes in 1897. Local hero Kit Calvert ensured its survival after a financial crisis in 1935 and built a new creamery in 1953. When this was closed down after nearly 40 years a vigorous local campaign saved the cheese. Production was restored using milk from local farms and this ensures the cheese has the traditional Wensleydale honey taste. The Creamery is now open to the public every day and has an interesting museum as well as a viewing gallery. The best time to see cheese making is between 10.30 am and 3 pm.

2. Cross the road to a path almost directly opposite, signed 'Youth Hostel ⅓ ML Mossy Lane ¼ ML'. Head up to a stile near the top left-hand corner of the field then continue along the left-hand side of four more fields to a lane.

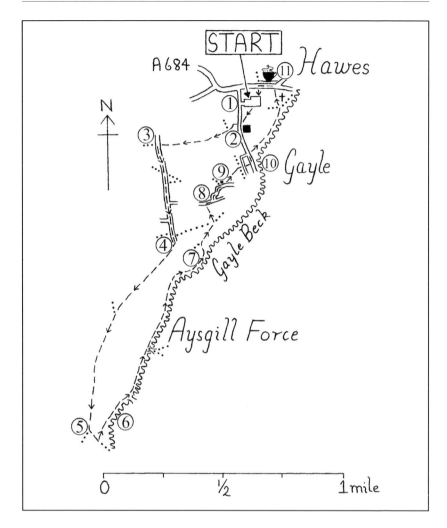

3. Turn left. Walk along the lane, continuing in the same direction at junctions on the left and right and when it is crossed by the Pennine Way.

4. The lane eventually bears right and after that continues as a track, signed 'Beggarmans Road 1'. Walk along the track for some ¾ mile.

5. Turn left through a gate onto a track which leads to the river below. Before reaching the river, leave the track on a signed footpath on the left which soon reaches the river bank.

6. Walk downstream. To begin with, the rather faint path is separated from the river by a wall and then it continues on the river bank. This is a delightful section of the walk, culminating in Aysgill Force.

7. About ½ mile downstream from the force, the path bears left away from the river and up some steps to a gated stile. Head across a field to another gated stile and over this turn left on the Pennine Way to reach a lane after two fields.

8. Turn right then bear left after 25 yards, still following the Pennine Way signs.

This is Gayle, a much older settlement than nearby Hawes to which it is now almost joined. It was an important centre of the hand knitting industry which survived here longer than almost anywhere else. Curved needles were used, one of which was supported in a sheath. The entire population knitted incessantly, women as they went about the house, children at school and men as they walked to work. The reason for this furious industry was to supplement the meagre income that could be made as contract labourers or working in the mill or lead mines.

9. Some 50 yards after a bungalow called 'Park View', take a paved path signed 'Pennine Way' on the left and follow it across two fields and between houses, crossing a road.

☕ **10.** When it emerges at a second road, turn left for 65 yards then take a path signed 'Pennine Way' on the right. This is again by the river with a view of some attractive cascades looking backwards. At Hawes church take a path to the left of the church to emerge on the main road through Hawes. Turn left and the teashop is on the right.

Hawes is the centre of Upper Wensleydale where the roads meet. The name derives from the old word for a pass and it was originally called The Hawes. Compared with some of the settlements hereabouts, however, it is not very old. There was little of it when places that are now quiet villages were important markets but as communications improved it grew into the busy centre we know today.

11. On leaving the teashop turn right through Hawes. Go up some steps signed 'Gayle and Creamery', beside the public conveniences on the left, back to the start.

Walk 7
BRIMHAM ROCKS

Brimham Rocks are the highlight of this easy and interesting walk which also explores Brimham Moor, particularly delightful in late summer when the heather is in full bloom. Brimham Rocks draw large crowds to marvel at their fantastical shapes. Few venture far away from the main attraction so the rest of this walk is very quiet. There are extensive views both east and west so a clear day is a must.

 The tea stop on this walk is more of a kiosk than a teashop but though the selection is limited, the quality is excellent. As well as cakes, sandwiches, soup and filled jacket potatoes are served. There is no accommodation indoors or tables outside – you take your tea and cake to a chosen spot among the rocks. From the beginning of April until late May it is open just at weekends except during the Easter holidays. Between late May and the beginning of September it is open every day and then reverts to weekend opening only until the end of October. The opening hours are

11 am until 5 pm. Telephone: 01423 780688.

There is no alternative source of refreshment on this walk.

DISTANCE: 3½ miles.

MAP: OS Explorer 298 Nidderdale.

STARTING POINT: The National Trust car park at Brimham Rocks (GR 208645). This is free for members.

HOW TO GET THERE: Follow the signs to Brimham Rocks from the B6165 Pateley Bridge-Harrogate road or the B6265 Pateley Bridge-Ripon road.

ALTERNATIVE STARTING POINT: The recommended car park is as close to tea as it is possible to get. Narrow roads and parking restrictions mean there is no other realistic starting place.

THE WALK

1. Return towards the entrance. Before reaching the public road, turn right on a track to Druids Cave Farm. Just before the National Trust boundary, turn left on a path to the road.

2. Cross the road and take a signed path directly opposite. Follow this across moorland and through a gate out of National Trust property to eventually join a surfaced farm track and continue in the same direction.

3. At a fork bear left through a metal gate to continue on the surfaced track.

4. Where a wood starts on the left, turn left on an unsigned fenced path, initially along the edge of the wood. Cross a stream then shortly ignore a path forking left and follow the path uphill to a gate into a field.

5. Through the gate continue in the same direction along the left-hand side of a field to a gate by a house. Walk along the drive, bearing left, and continue over two cattle grids to eventually arrive at a lane.

The large golf ball shapes you can see in the distance on your left are Menwith Hill, a communications station.

6. Take a narrow and possibly rather overgrown path directly across the road climbing to the rocks ahead. The path leads up through the rocks, bearing slightly right, to reach a narrow cross path about 20 yards beyond the rocks. Turn left along this to a T-junction after about 100 yards. Turn sharp right and follow the path through the heather. A group of rocks comes into view ahead and the path leads towards them. As the path approaches the

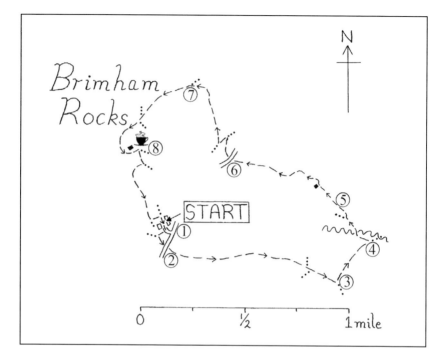

rocks, follow the 'main', though none the less very narrow path as it bears left to a T-junction with a path leading down from the outcrop

The vegetation we see today is not entirely natural. The old name for the area was 'birnbeam', of which 'Brimham' is a corruption. Beam in this context means tree, suggesting that the moor was once heavily wooded. The trees were cleared by the monks of Fountains who once farmed the estate. The dominant plant on the moor now is heather. If you examine it closely you will find that there are actually three different species present – true heather or ling, bell heather and cross leaved heath. They are supposed to like slightly different conditions with cross leaved heath preferring wetter surroundings than true heather and bell heather being found in the driest circumstances but they often grow intermixed, as they do here. The ling has few leaves on the main shoots and the short side shoots bear four dense ranks of small leaves. The flowers are single and pale, pinkish purple. The bell heather has leaves which can be tinged with bronze and curled over to protect the underside of the leaf. The leaves grow in a whorl or ring of three up the stem, each whorl giving rise to a leafy shoot. The flowers are a bit bigger than true heather, darker purple and are carried in a head or loose spike. The cross leafed heather has its leaves in whorls of four and they look quite ghrey because they are downy. The flowers are the largest of the three species, pink in colour and occur in a tight cluster at tips of the twigs. To help maintain the grouse population, the heather is cut or burned in strips in rotation. This ensures there is heather of different ages – the young shoots are eaten by the birds while the older plants provide nesting sites. Sundews can be found in the wetter areas. These insectivorous plants have modified leaves with sticky hairs to trap insects. These are then digested by juices produced by the leaves to provide the nitrogen needed for the plant's growth but in short supply in went areas on poor soil.

7. Turn left on this narrow path. It is worth going up to the rocks for the magnificent view but please be very sure to leave them by the right path – it is very easy to take the wrong one and get lost here. To continue, follow the main path, eventually bearing right to the main body of the rocks in the trees ahead. Bear right again through the amazing natural sculptures to the front of the information centre and the tea kiosk is just ahead.

Note: There is a maze of paths around here so don't worry if you miss the route. Make your way to the building which is the information centre and the tea kiosk is just by it.

These amazing columns of eroded millstone grit have attracted tourists since at least the 18th century. Many have been given names, such as the Crown, Anvil and Dancing Bear and of course there is the inevitable Lovers' Leap. At one time the story was that they had been carved by Druids but the geological truth is just as fantastic. The rock was laid down about 300 million years ago as deposits of sand and mud washed down by rivers. They were then buried deep in the Earth's crust and cemented into rock. Later earth movements exposed the millstone grit to the elements which carved these natural sculptures. There is a very good audio-visual display in the information centre describing in more detail how they came to be formed.

8. There are several possible routes back to the car park so choose your own! However, a good way, which passes many interesting rocks and view points, is as follows. With your back to the picnic area in front of the information centre there are two major paths ahead. Take the one directly in front, marked by a post. After 130 yards turn right on a wide path that wends through the rocks with many side paths to the various formations and view points. After about ¼ mile turn left into the car park.

Walk 8
PATELEY BRIDGE

This short walk approaches Pateley Bridge by the aptly named 'Panorama Path' which has sweeping views over Nidderdale and the town. This is a busy and bustling place whose Main Street has many interesting and individual shops. One claims to be the oldest sweetshop in the world! The return after tea is an easy stroll on the banks of the river Nidd. These two delightful paths are linked by a climb. However, this is made easier because you tackle it in two parts, one bit at the beginning and one at the end.

 Housed in an old stone pump house, Wildings is a charming and very popular traditional teashop with an attractive terrace overlooking the river Nidd as it wends its way through Pateley Bridge. They offer a good selection of most tempting cakes including parkin, fruit cake and flapjack. Wildings is also an excellent lunch stop offering a range of sandwiches served with a generous salad or a choice of pancakes with sweet or savoury fillings as well as full meals. They are open between 9.30 am and 5 pm from Wednesday to Sunday throughout the year. Between March and October they open on Tuesdays as well and on Bank Holiday Mondays. Telephone: 01423 711152. When the teashop is closed there are several establishments in Pateley Bridge serving refreshments.

DISTANCE: 2½ miles.

MAP: OS Explorer 298 Nidderdale.

STARTING POINT: The layby on the east side of the B6265 near its junction with the B6165 (GR 173648).

HOW TO GET THERE: From the B6165 Harrogate-Pateley Bridge road 1 mile east of Pateley Bridge, take the B6265 Ripon road to the layby, 100 yards along on the right.

ALTERNATIVE STARTING POINT: If you want to visit the teashop at the beginning or end of your walk, start at one of the well signed car parks in Pateley Bridge. Wildings overlooks the river just before the bridge. You will then start the walk at point 5.

THE WALK

1. Walk along the B6265, away from the junction with the B6165, for 200 yards.

2. Turn left on a public bridleway, signed 'Knott Panorama Walk'. Follow this as it climbs through trees, forking left at a junction. As the path levels out, excellent views open up on the left, justifying the name of the 'Panorama Path'. Continue past a house and along the track between walls.

3. At a lane turn right to continue in the same direction, soon passing a public bridleway on the right. Carry on ahead along what is now more of a surfaced track, passing a cemetery on the right and then going downhill.

4. At a T-junction with a road turn right and follow the main road through Pateley Bridge to the river. Do not cross the bridge but turn left along Nidd Walk to the teashop on the right.

The name 'Pateley' probably comes from pate, an old word for a badger. The town's varied and interesting past is recounted in its award winning Nidderdale Museum, to be found in the Council Offices and open every day from Easter to September and on Sunday afternoons in winter (telephone: 01423 711225). Particularly fascinating are the reconstructed shops and offices. Built of dark millstone grit, Pateley Bridge can have a dour aspect on a gloomy day but this it lightened by the lovely floral displays in public places.

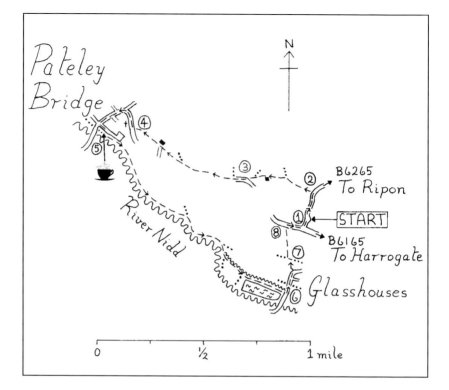

5. Turn right out of the teashop and immediately right again to a path by the river. Turn left and follow this level path for about a mile.

6. At a road turn left. Some 50 yards after passing Harwell Close on the right, take a path on the left up some stone steps and follow the paved path up to a track.

Glasshouses is first mentioned in 1387 but remained a small hamlet of handloom weavers' cottages until the Metcalfe family transferred their flax business here in 1828. They built a reservoir to ensure a reliable water supply for the 32 foot diameter wheel that drove the machinery, together with houses and other amenities for the workers.

7. Turn left. After 25 yards, just before Hollins Cottage, turn right on a path between wall and fence and, after a gate, along the left-hand side of a field.

8. At a road turn right and then left, back to the start.

Walk 9
BOLTON ABBEY

*T*his is a highly recommended short walk that everyone will enjoy. The scenery is some of the best in the Dales, especially the view of Bolton Abbey as you approach it from an unusual direction. The Abbey itself is fascinating to explore. This is rounded off by a really good tea before a short stroll on the banks of the river Wharfe prior to returning home. All in all, this walk makes a delightful afternoon's expedition..

 Bolton Abbey Tea Cottage is a traditional teashop with a lovely garden and terrace giving an outstanding view out over the Abbey and river. The building was originally part of a tithe barn and later two small cottages, occupied until 1977. The interior has been skilfully converted and is very attractive with modern decor complementing the old building. There is an excellent selection of delicious cakes, temptingly displayed. For lunch

45

there is a good choice of sandwiches served with salad and crisps as well as daily specials. Tasty home-made soup is welcome in winter, as is the hot chocolate with marshmallows, whipped cream and buttons. The Tea Cottage is open from 10 am every day, closing at 4 pm in the winter and later in summer. Telephone: 01756 710495. Website: www.boltonabbey.com/shopandeat/food/tea_cottage.

DISTANCE: 3 miles

MAP: OL2 Yorkshire Dales Southern & Western areas.

STARTING POINT: Bolton Bridge, where there is parking for half a dozen cars. (Grid reference 071530) If this is full, go along the A59 towards Harrogate for about a mile then turn left, at a No Through Road sign. A bend has been taken out of the main road and there is space to park here on the old road. You will now pick up the route at point 6: with your back to the main road, go to the left hand end of the old road.

HOW TO GET THERE: At a roundabout on the A59 take the B6160, signed for Bolton Abbey. Immediately after crossing a stone bridge, turn right to a small parking area in bays at the roadside.

ALTERNATIVE STARTING POINT: If you want to visit the teashop at the beginning or end of your walk, start at Bolton Abbey where there is ample parking. The teashop is across the road from the car park (charge). You will then begin the walk at point 11.

THE WALK

1. With your back to the parking area turn left to walk along the old road. When this ends carry on to join the A59 for 200 yards.

2. Turn right along a lane signed 'Beamsley ½'.

3. Immediately after the first house on the left, turn left on a track. Follow the track until it eventually peters out in a field. Continue ahead to a gate by a barn to pick up a path on the river bank.

4. Turn left, upriver.

5. When the wall on the left starts to rise follow it up to a stile in the corner. (Alternatively continue on the riverbank for about 50 yards and an easier path leads backwards uphill to this stile.) Walk along the left-hand side of two fields to the A59.

6. Cross the road and turn right. At the top of the slope turn left on a

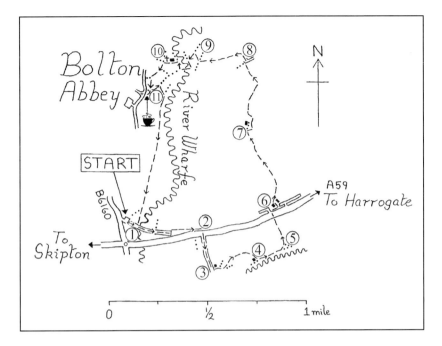

footpath signed 'Storiths'. Walk between buildings and over a cattle grid on a surfaced track. Follow this uphill and over a second cattle grid, heading towards a farm.

7. Immediately after passing through a gateway, turn right to walk with a wall on the right. At the end of the field turn left to continue round the field to a gate. Continue across the next field to a gated squeeze stile and then bear left down to another stile. Now walk along the left-hand side of the next field to a further stile and then head half right across the next field to a stile by a gate. Keep ahead along the right-hand side of a further field to a gate on the right. Bear left to a stile near a gate on to a lane.

8. Take the track opposite signed 'Priory Bridge ¼ ML'. When the track ends, continue ahead on a walled path and follow this to a cross paths where there is a superb view of Bolton Abbey and the river Wharfe.

From this vantage point the magnificent situation of Bolton Abbey can be fully appreciated. Though it is commonly called Bolton Abbey, it should really be referred to as Bolton Priory. The distinction between the two is as follows. An abbey was inhabited by monks who were more insular and had private religious services. A

47

priory, on the other hand, was made up of ordained priests, living together as monks but more involved in the world and ministering to the needs of local people who were allowed to attend Mass. They ran schools and hospitals, sheltered travellers and served as parish priests. This activity was sustained by an arduous round of prayer for which they rose at 2 am. The Augustinian priors settled here in 1154 on land given to them by Alice de Romilly of Skipton Castle when a site at Embsay they had received from her mother proved to be unsuitable. Over the years the Priory was constructed piecemeal as funds were available to pay the travelling masons. By 1220 much of the church and domestic buildings had been completed but work was still in progress when the end came with the Dissolution in 1539.

9. Turn right and follow the main path down to a lower path. Turn left. Cross the river, using the footbridge or stepping stones. Turn right and walk up to the ruins and through to the church.

At the Dissolution the priors were turned out, the lead stripped from the roof and the furnishings taken away. However, the nave of the priory church was spared as a place of worship for local people. It still fulfils this role today and has therefore undergone many changes and additions down the centuries. Much information is available within and particularly worth seeing is the symbolic painting on the East wall, executed in the 19th century when the wall was rebuilt. The west tower, left unfinished at the Dissolution, has been roofed in modern times to form an entrance porch with outstanding acoustic properties. The estate was bought by the Clifford family and a descendent married into the Dukes of Devonshire, who still own it today. Gradually all the rest of the priory became a romantic ruin; one which inspired Turner, amongst others – he painted Bolton Abbey in 1809.

10. From the church turn left along the drive. Take the second path on the left through a gate and walk across to a gate into the teashop garden, crossing a surfaced path.

11. Leave the garden by the same gate you entered and return to the surfaced path. Turn right then soon turn right again to pick up a path along the river bank. Follow this back to Bolton Bridge and the start.

As you head down towards the river look on the left for some depressions. These are the remains of the monastic fish ponds. The Reverend W. Carr, who laid out the paths further upriver in the early 19th century (see walk 10) bred the famous Craven heifer here. This notable beast weighed 312 stones 8 lbs (1956 kg) and is remembered in the name of many pubs. The word 'Craven' here refers to the area where it originated and not to any timidity.

Walk 10
THE STRID

The word 'strid' apparently comes from an old word for turmoil. While this is true of the waters of the Wharfe as they pass through the rocky defile, this deservedly popular walk is more likely to calm jangled nerves than plunge you into chaos. The woods surrounding the Wharfe in these reaches are outstanding and have been recognised as a Site of Special Scientific Interest. The river is infinitely varied and The Strid itself an interesting phenomenon. The outward and return paths are very different, the outward one being mainly high above the river with views down to it while the return is along the river bank.

The description of teashop walk is certainly true for this route with two to choose from, one at the start and one about two thirds of the way round. Cavendish Pavilion, just under a mile downstream from the Strid, has served teas to visitors for very many years. It offers a good selection of cakes as well as full meals and snacks. Its position is outstanding, overlooking the Wharfe, and it has plenty of tables outside to take advantage of this, some under a veranda. The Pavilion is open every day except Christmas Day from 10 am, closing at 4 pm in the winter and 5 pm in the summer. Telephone: 01756 710245. Website: www.cavendishpavilion.co.uk

Strid Wood Tearoom overlooks the car park where this walk starts. It is deservedly popular with visitors to this lovely area and similarly serves excellent cakes and scones, as well as sandwiches and daily specials for lunch. The Tearoom is open every day except Christmas Day between 9.30 am and 4.30 pm. Telephone: 01756 711745. Website: www.stridwoodtearooms.co.uk

DISTANCE: 4 miles.

MAP: OL2 Yorkshire Dales Southern & Western areas.

STARTING POINT: Strid Wood car park (GR 058563), for which there is a charge.

HOW TO GET THERE: The entrance to the car park is signed from the B6160 Bolton Abbey-Burnsall road.

ALTERNATIVE STARTING POINT: If you want to visit the teashop at the beginning or end of your walk, start at Cavendish Pavilion where there is a large car park. From the B6160 Bolton Abbey – Burnsall road, just by the Cavendish Memorial, turn down the drive leading to the Riverside car park. The teashop is just beyond the car park. You will then begin the walk at point 5.

THE WALK

1. Take the track from the rear of the car park, next to the teashop, for 250 yards.

2. Turn left on a path marked with green arrows and follow this down to the river bank. Turn left upriver as far as the first bridge.

This bridge looks more important than it is. It has only ever been a footbridge and its castellated appearance was created just to add to the river scene.

(Note: if you want to extend the walk, continue along the river bank for about ½ mile to cross the river at the next bridge, Barden Bridge)

3. Cross the river and turn right, back downstream, soon climbing above the river. There are several seats, some in a substantial shelter, strategically placed to admire the view.

This woodland has been managed for human enjoyment and recreation for nearly 200 years – many of the paths this route uses were laid out in the early years of the 19th century by the Reverend William Carr with carefully arranged stopping points and views. The result of this management is a superb richness of wildlife, recognised in the area's designation as a Site of Special Scientific Interest, and the coloured arrows are signs for the several nature trails laid out to help the public enjoy this outstanding woodland. Walking here is a joy in any season – the spring is best for wildflowers including wonderful drifts of bluebells, the autumn for colours and winter for views.

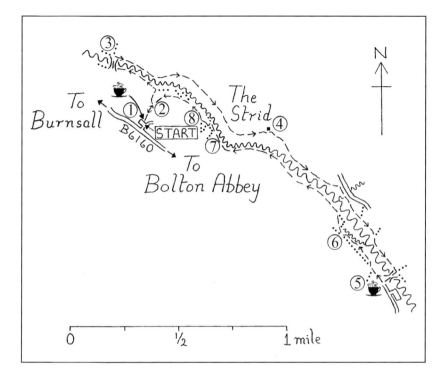

There are two main species of oak found in Britain – the common oak and the
durmast oak. They are not that easy to tell apart and often hybridise where they
grow together. The easiest distinguishing features are that the durmast oak has
acorns with no stalks, or at most a short, thick stalk, whereas the common oak bears
its fruits on longer stalks. For this reason the durmast oak is sometimes called the
sessile oak, the word sessile meaning without a stalk. However just to confuse, the
sessile oak has longer leaf stalks than the common oak!

☕ **4.** Stay on the path as it leads downhill to the river. Follow the path
downriver, leaving the river briefly to cross a stream at a footbridge beside a
lane. Cross the river at the first footbridge to the teashop.

*The teashop is called the Cavendish Pavilion. These woods are part of the Duke of
Devonshire's estate. Frederick Charles Cavendish was the son of the 7th Duke of
Devonshire and appointed Chief Secretary for Ireland in 1882. A few hours after
his arrival in Dublin he was stabbed to death, together with his under-secretary
T. H. Burke, while walking in Phoenix Park. On the road just by the entrance to the
Pavilion car park is an elaborate fountain erected as a memorial.*

51

5. From the teashop take the path upriver. About 100 yards after a gate across the path, bear right on a riverside path marked by a purple arrow and follow this until it rejoins the main path.

As you go along this path you might catch a whiff of sulphur in the air. It comes from a spring once reputed to have medicinal properties.

6. Turn right and carry on along the main path.

7. Soon after a prominent information board, bear right to view The Strid. You will be guided to it by the sound. Return to the main path and turn right. When the path shortly forks bear right, ignoring the left fork signed 'Barden Bridge Strid Wood car park'.

Notices draw the dangers of The Strid to visitors' attention. The river has eroded a deep chasm here through which the water surges and boils. Apart from the turbulence of the water the currents are such that anything that falls in apparently does not surface for several days. Unwary souls who thought they could jump across have been killed. Legend has it that one casualty was the Boy of Egremond, heir to the great Romilly estates and in her grief his mother Alice founded Bolton Priory. Historical fact is more prosaic, however, as his signature appears on the endowment deed (see walk 9).

8. At a T-junction turn right. When the path forks bear left then left again, away from the river, signed 'Strid Wood Car Park'. Pause at the top of the hill to enjoy the magnificent view up the Wharfe and then continue on the main path to the car park, rejoining the outward route for the last 250 yards.

Turner's View

Walk 11
HEBDEN AND BURNSALL

This walk is very easy going with just one climb of any significance and that is only about 100 feet. The walk starts in Hebden and heads out on a level path across the small fields above the river Wharfe. These are mainly separated by stone walls and so there are unrivalled opportunities to review the many designs of stile. The route then drops down into the valley and there follows a delightful 2 mile stretch along the bank of the river, crossing it at an old suspension footbridge. After tea, the return leg makes its way by fields, woods and river bank back to the start.

The name of the Wharfe View Tea Rooms exactly describes its position and in summer there are tables outside to enjoy the prospect. A full range of teatime goodies is served including a tempting array of cakes, alluringly displayed on a trolley. For lunch a number of snacks and full meals are available, among them meat and potato pie, sandwiches and salads. It is open throughout the year from 9.30 am to 5 pm, just closing on Thursday and Friday. Telephone: 01756 720237.

An excellent alternative, especially before or after the walk, is the Old School Tea Room in Hebden. You could fortify yourself before the walk with their traditional breakfast, served until 11.30 am, and for tea there is a delicious selection of cakes. Should you visit at lunchtime, there is a good choice for all appetites from sandwiches and salads to steak and ale pie. There are some tables outside in what was once the school playground. They are open every day between 10 am and 5 pm. Telephone: 01756 753778. Website: www.theoldschooltearoom.com

DISTANCE: 5 miles.

MAP: OL2 Yorkshire Dales Southern & Western areas.

STARTING POINT: Hebden Village playground, next to Old School Tea Room on the left (GR 026630).

HOW TO GET THERE: Hebden straddles the B6265 Grassington-Pateley Bridge road. At Hebden turn into the village, signed 'Burnsall 2¼'. There are several spots where it is possible to park without causing inconvenience to local residents.

ALTERNATIVE STARTING POINT: If you want to visit the teashop at the beginning or end of your walk, start in Burnsall where there is a car park by the river (charge). The teashop is across the road. You will then start the walk at point 6.

The walk

1. With your back to the playground, turn left through the village. Just past the Old School Tea Room on the left, take the first road on the right up to the church.

Hebden is an ancient settlement, recorded in the Domesday Book as Hebedene, which literally means Rose Hip Valley.

2. Follow the path ahead, signed 'Linton Falls 1½ML and Grassington 2ML'. At the time of writing, it is not visible on the ground but goes ahead across two fields to a stone stile. Over the stile continue in the same direction along the right-hand side of a field to a further stile. When the wall on the right ends, continue in the same direction to yet another stile. Over this stile, turn right to walk on the right-hand side of a broken wall to a small gate in the far left corner.

3. Continue on this path, which is not very apparent on the ground but is easy to follow from stile to stile, with the help of the signs. The path eventually crosses a farm track and goes to the left of two barns. Soon after this the river below comes into view and the path heads down towards it, joining a farm track for the last 250 yards.

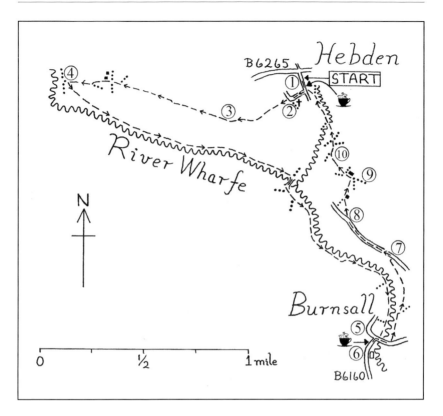

4. Just before a junction with another track, turn left on a broad, grassy path, heading towards a small wooden bridge and onwards to the river bank. Follow the path along the river bank for about a mile, then cross the river at a suspension footbridge and continue in the same direction on the opposite bank for a further mile.

The river Wharfe, one of the best fishing rivers in the North of England, rises high on the moors of Cam Pasture and flows in a broad glacial valley past a series of ancient villages. The long distance Dales Way Footpath, from Ilkley in Yorkshire to Bowness in Cumbria, follows the river bank along this stretch.

☕ **5.** At a stone road bridge over the river, turn right and cross the road to the teashop.

The picturesque village of Burnsall is well worth a wander round. It was founded over 1,000 years ago by the Angles and the church, largely rebuilt in the reign of

Henry VIII, has some ancient remnants including a couple of hogback tombstones dating from the 9th and 10th centuries and fragments of crosses of the same date. The main street today wends its way between 17th and 18th-century houses, many with attractive mullioned windows.

Burnsall has its own Dick Whittington. Sir William Craven was a 16th/17th-century local boy who made a fortune in drapery and became Lord Mayor of London. He spent some of his fortune on his native village, including the church and handsome Grammar School. This continued as a grammar school until 1876 and is now the local primary school.

The date of the famous Feast Sports is worked out by a complicated formula, being held on the first Saturday following the first Sunday after August 12th. They have been held since the reign of Elizabeth I and are said to be the oldest in the country.

6. From the teashop cross the stone bridge over the river and immediately turn left on a path, signed 'Scuff Road ½ML', on the river bank. This soon bears right to a ladder stile over a wall. Now bear half left uphill, ignoring a path straight ahead up to a gate. Follow the path above a stand of trees to a road.

The bridge was built in 1612 and is another example of the generosity of William Craven. The river Wharfe may look peaceful most of the time but it can be wild and turbulent when it is in spate after heavy rain or when snow melts and this bridge has stood the test of time, unlike its predecessors.

7. Turn left along the road.

8. After ¼ mile take a path on the right, signed 'Hebden'. This is not apparent on the ground at the time of writing but goes half left to a gate to the left of a farm building. Go through the gate onto a surfaced track and turn right.

9. At a farm bear left between farm buildings and then head straight across a field to a stile in a stone wall. Go across the bottom corner of a field, slightly left for 10 yards to a substantial stone stile and ahead to a track.

10. Turn right along the track. Just after a track joins on the left, before a gate, bear left and cross a small stream, using stone slabs, and then cross a larger stream at a footbridge. Continue ahead, through a wooden kissing-gate, and follow the path up to emerge in Hebden. Turn right, back to the start.

Walk 12
GRASSINGTON

This delightful short walk explores one of the largest stretches of deciduous, broad-leaved woodland left in the Yorkshire Dales – Grass Wood, a National Nature Reserve – before visiting Grassington and an outstanding teashop. The return leg along the river Wharfe is very attractive and there are many spots where you will be tempted to linger.

Springfield Tea Rooms, 51 Main Street, is one of many places where you can have tea in Grassington, as you would expect in an attractive and interesting village which attracts large numbers of visitors every year. It is a charming traditional teashop which is exceptionally walker-friendly and will fill your flask for you if you need refreshment for the rest of the walk. There are a couple of tables outside, an excellent place to watch the world go by. For tea there are a good selection of cakes or scones served with jam and cream with a choice of sandwiches or filled jacket potatoes for lunch. Springfield's is open throughout the year from 9.30 am until 4 pm every day except Monday and Tuesday (open Bank Holidays). Telephone: 01756 753208.

DISTANCE: 4 miles.
MAP: OL2 Yorkshire Dales Southern & Western areas.
STARTING POINT: Grass Wood car park on the Conistone-Grassington road (GR 985652).
HOW TO GET THERE: From the B6160, the main road through Wharfedale, just south of Kilnsey, take a minor road signed 'Conistone ½'. Turn right in Conistone, signed 'Grassington 3'. After about 1¾ miles look for the entrance to a small parking area on the left opposite a ladder stile over a fence on the right – not at all easy to spot! From the B6265 in Grassington take a minor road signed 'Conistone 3 Kettlewell 6¼'. Follow this lane for just under 1½ miles to an unsigned car park on the right.
ALTERNATIVE STARTING POINT: If you want to visit the teashop at the beginning or end of your walk, start in the large public car park by the National Park information centre at Grassington. Turn left out of the car park. To visit the teashop before your walk turn right up Main Street and the Springfield's is near the top, on the left and then retrace your steps to the junction. Otherwise, continue ahead to join the walk at point 8..

THE WALK
1. Facing the road, look for a stile over the right-hand fence of the car park. Over this turn right and follow the path uphill to a T-junction with a crosspath.

If you had visited the Yorkshire Dales 3,000 years ago, after the end of the last Ice Age but before humans had much influence, the landscape would have been very different. The bare hills we see today would almost all have been clothed in mixed deciduous woodland – the temperate rain forest. Human activity has removed it all and today there are very few extensive areas of woodland left – Grass Wood is one of them. There are remains of wood drying hearths that show it was exploited as a source of fuel for the local lead industry in the 17th, 18th and 19th centuries. In 1989 it was bought by the Woodlands Trust who manage it to enhance wildlife interest by encouraging a diversity of habitats.

2. Turn left. Bear right at a path junction and then follow the main path along the hillside, ignoring a path on the left after 70 yards and on the right after a further 30 yards.

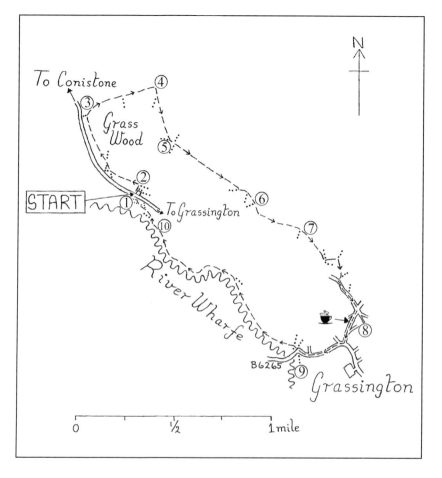

3. At a T-junction with a crosstrack turn right and follow the track as it climbs gently through the wood. The trees on the left soon thin out to give superb views up Wharfedale, in particular of Kilnsey Crag. When the track bends sharply right after about ¼ mile, continue in the same direction on a path.

4. After a further ¼ mile the path bends sharp right and continues uphill. Ignore a grassy ride on the right about 150 yards after the bend. All the climbing is now over and the next part of the route follows a delightful level path through the wood.

5. At a T-junction turn left along a crosspath. The path soon comes to a signed crosspaths. Continue ahead, signed 'Grassington', and follow the main path, now downhill, ignoring all paths on the right, to leave the wood at a stile.

As you go downhill, watch out for a sign on the right indicating the site of a Brigantian settlement dating from about the first century AD. There is little to see, just some humps among the vegetation. The Brigantes offered stiff resistance to the Romans, though imperial might eventually prevailed here as elsewhere.

6. Cross a field to a gap in a wall and continue across the next field to the right-hand of two gates at the far end. The gate gives onto a walled track. When this turns right go up some steps in the left-hand corner and over a stile.

☕ **7.** The path now bears half right up to a gated stile. Cross a track to a second stile then turn left to a squeeze stile on the right. Go across a field to a gate onto a track. Turn right to reach a T-junction with a lane on the outskirts of Grassington. Turn left. At the crossroads by the Town Hall, turn right and the teashop is a few yards ahead on the right.

Though Grassington is an ancient centre for the dale with a market charter dating back to the 13th century, the village we see today is largely the product of the successful lead mining industry of the 18th and 19th centuries. The textile industry was important at this time too, driven by water power. Just as the lead industry started to decline, the railway arrived, bringing tourists and maintaining the village's prosperity. Grassington once had its own rail link to the line between Skipton and Threshfield and is well worth exploring with many interesting buildings. A leaflet is available to guide you round the village.

8. After visiting the teashop, continue on down Main Street. At the bottom, turn right then follow the main road round, signed 'Cracoe 3½ Skipton 9¼'.

9. Just before a bridge over the river, turn right and follow a path down to the river bank. Walk upstream for about a mile, soon passing Ghaistrill's Strid where the river falls rapidly through a narrow channel.

10. After about a mile, the path climbs steeply away from the river. The path forks at the top. Take the right-hand branch and follow the path along the top of the valley. Ignore the first path on the right then take the second on the right which leads to a stile giving onto the road opposite the start.

Walk 13
HUBBERHOLME AND BUCKDEN

A short though energetic walk, the effort expended on two short sharp climbs is fully repaid by long level or downhill stretches with fabulous views of Upper Wharfedale. The teashop at Buckden is ideally positioned to take advantage of the idyllic position of the village and the return leg is mostly on a lovely path by the river Wharfe.

Buckden Village Restaurant, located in a 17th-century miner's cottage next to the shop and post office, is perfectly positioned at the head of Wharfedale with several tables outside to appreciate the superb view. A good range of cakes and other teatime temptations is served as well as full meals and sandwiches or filled jacket potatoes for a lighter lunch. It is open every day except Wednesday throughout the year from 10 am until 5 pm. Telephone: 01756 760257.

When the teashop is closed the Buck Inn in Buckden, noted for its food, serves lunches and afternoon teas.

DISTANCE: 4½ miles.

MAP: OL30 Yorkshire Dales Northern & Central areas.

STARTING POINT: The bridge over the river Wharfe in Hubberholme (GR 926782).

HOW TO GET THERE: From the B6160, the main road through Wharfedale, at Buckden, take a minor road signed 'Hubberholme 1¼'. At the George turn right over the river to a parking spot just ahead by the river on the right. Should that be full, there is another, smaller one just before the George.

ALTERNATIVE STARTING POINT: If you want to visit the teashop at the beginning or end of your walk, start at Buckden where there is ample parking in the public car park. The teashop is just across the road from the entrance to the car park. You will then begin the walk at point 5.

THE WALK

The hamlet of Hubberholme is in a superb setting, nestling in the hills with the river Wharfe splashing and babbling under the ancient bridge that links the church and pub. This lovely spot is a favourite with many visitors to the Dales, including the Bradford born author J.B. Priestley. His ashes were scattered in the churchyard. The George was once the vicarage and was owned by the church until 1965. The field behind is let for the benefit of the poor of the parish and on New Year's day the Hubberholme Parliament meets here to auction the tenancy. Local farmers bid for the grazing, the rent going to the needy of the parish.

1. Take the track next to the church, signed 'Deepdale 2½ML Yockenthwaite 1¾ML Cray 2ML'. When this forks behind the church, bear right, signed 'Scar House & Cray', and follow the track up to the house.

2. Turn right behind the house then left on a track between walls. After 40 yards turn right on a footpath, signed 'Cray', initially across a rocky area and then above some woods. Follow this path, with outstanding views down Wharfedale, as it contours round the hillside and then descends by some farm buildings to emerge on the road at Cray by the White Lion.

3. Cross the road and take the footpath opposite, signed 'Cray High Bridge ½ Buckden 1½', crossing a stream using stepping stones. Follow the path up by a wall and then bear right away from the wall to a gate onto a crosspath.

☕ **4.** Turn right. Follow this path along the hillside and then down to emerge in the car park at Buckden. Cross the car park to the teashop just opposite the entrance.

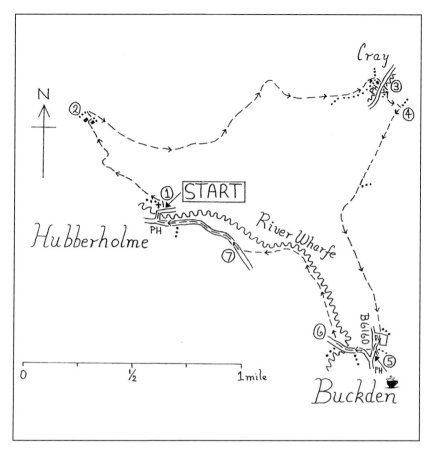

Buckden stands at the northern end of Wharfedale, just before it turns sharply west and changes its name to Langstrothdale. Its name and that of the pub, the Buck Inn, tell of its origin as a Norman hunting lodge for Langstrothdale Chase.

5. Cross the road outside the teashop and take a path by the green to the Hubberholme road. Turn right.

6. Just after a bridge over the river, turn right over a stile on a path signed 'Hubberholme 1¼ML'. Follow this to the river bank and then continue by the river until the path swings away from the bank back to the lane.

7. Turn right and follow the lane back to the start.

Walk 14
KIRKBY MALHAM AND AIRTON

This walk explores Airedale below Malham and is a gem, so easily ignored as visitors rush past on their way to the well-known sites of Malham. The route starts in one charming Dales village and wends its way to a second, with an excellent farm shop and tearoom. A little climbing is involved but nothing too strenuous and the reward is a series of outstanding views. The return is a section of the Pennine Way by the river Aire and is a delight.

 Town End Farm Shop Tearoom is in a converted barn with huge windows to enjoy the view. The flagged floor and sturdy pine tables perfectly capture the ambience of this area. There is a tempting display of cakes on a sideboard to choose from, and for lunch there are sandwiches and jacket potatoes with tasty fillings such as smoked chicken with fruity mayonnaise. They are open throughout the year every day except Monday (open Bank Holidays) from 9.30 am (10 am on Sundays) until 5 pm. Telephone: 01729 830902. Website: www.townendfarmshop.co.uk

DISTANCE: 3½ miles.

MAP: OL2 Yorkshire Dales Southern & Western areas.

STARTING POINT: The Victoria Inn, Kirkby Malham (GR 894609).

HOW TO GET THERE: From the main square in Settle take a minor road signed 'Airton 6 Gargrave 12 Barnoldswick 20' then follow the signs to Kirkby Malham. At a T-junction as you enter Kirby Malham, turn right. There are several spots where a car can be left without causing inconvenience, notably at the side of the lane signed 'Hanlith ½ only' opposite the Victoria Inn.

ALTERNATIVE STARTING POINT: If you wish to visit the teashop at the beginning or end of your walk, start at the farm shop on the edge of Airton, though permission must be sought before leaving a car for an extended period. You will then start the walk at point 7.

THE WALK

1. With your back to the Victoria Inn, turn right along the lane to the church. Opposite the church, turn left along a footpath signed 'Otterburn 2¾ML' and follow the path across the stream and uphill through two gates.

The name of the village (Kirkby translates as church place) suggests that there was a church here when the Danes came in the 9th and 10th centuries, though the Domesday Book refers to this area as wasteland. The present building is basically late 15th-century. In the 12th century, Adam, son of Adam de Giggleswick, owned the manor of Kirkby and he gave it to the Abbey of Our Lady at West Dereham in Norfolk who provided the vicars until the dissolution of the monasteries. All but three of the incumbents from this period were born in Norfolk but came to serve in this remote corner of Yorkshire. The last, John Downham, arrived in 1509, and lived on in charge of the parish after the dissolution of his old abbey until his death in 1550. A tall marble cross marks one grave in the churchyard. Colonel and Mrs John Harrison were separated for long periods due to John's frequent service overseas and Helen decided that water should separate them in death as it had so often in life. She therefore arranged that the small stream which runs across this grave plot should separate their final resting places. Helen died in 1890 and was buried on the south side of the stream. John died in 1900, but it was found that the north side was impenetrable rock – so John was buried on the south side with Helen after all.

2. Through the second gate bear right up towards a wood, eventually walking with the wood on the right, then to a stile on to a track.

3. Cross the track and a stile and now bear slightly left across the field to find a bridge over a stream to the right of a line of trees. Keep ahead to a stile over

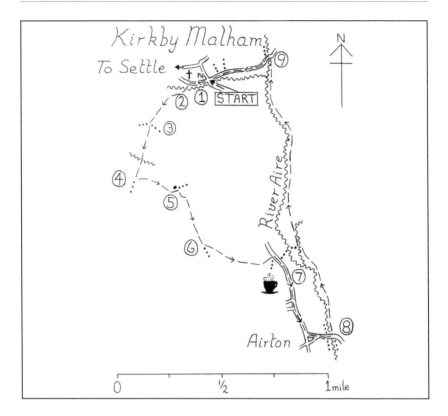

a wall just before a gate then continue with the wall on the left for 120 yards to a gate.

4. Turn left, signed 'Airton ½ML', but do not believe the sign: it is about ½ mile to Kirkby Malham and more like a mile to Airton. Head slightly left downhill to shortly walk with a fence on the left to a gate then go ahead a few yards to a barn on the left.

Look left for a superb long-range view of Malham Cove, visited on Walk 15.

5. Turn right through a small gate beside a metal field gate. Over the stile go ahead along the left-hand side of three fields, losing the view of Malham Cove and Airton coming into view as you go over the rise.

☕ **6.** In the fourth field bear left to a stile in the far left corner. Walk along the left-hand side of two small fields and across a third to a gate. Now cut across the corner of the next field and walk along the right-hand side of the same field to a road. Turn right to the teashop in the farm shop on the right.

7. Return to the road and turn right into Airton. At the village green turn left and walk down to a bridge over the river.

Airton had strong Quaker connections and there is still no pub in the village. The Meeting House is still in use and the stables next door, built for worshippers to leave their horses, have been converted into a bunk-house popular with people walking the Pennine Way. The large building overlooking the river was Airton Mill. Originally the site of a corn mill, it had many uses including cotton spinning. In 1918, A.E. Jackson of Blackburn, started Airton Engineering Co. He installed an electric generator driven by the water wheel and supplied domestic lighting to all the houses in the village as well as street lighting. This was financed by fund-raising whist drives and collections from every householder. A workman at the mill was responsible for the maintenance and keeping the supply going. His day's work finished at 10.30 pm when the lights were turned off. In 1942, Reckitt & Coleman bought the mill and moved their Dettol production, from the heavily bombed Hull area to the peace of Airton. There was at least one accident when all the fish were killed by phenol leaking into the river. People collected some of them and tried to make them edible by soaking them in clean water in the bath for a few days, but when they cooked them they still tasted of Dettol so they were boiled up and fed to animals. Industrial use ended in 1972 and the mill was sold and converted into flats.

8. At the far side of the bridge turn left on a riverside path signed 'Pennine Way Hanlith 1\frac 13/ml'. Follow the way-marked Pennine Way for about a mile, mostly by the river, to the next stone bridge across the river (not the wooden footbridge after about ½ mile).

The river Aire starts at Malham Tarn (see Walk 15) and after a few hundred yards it vanishes through deep fissures in its limestone bed at a place appropriately called 'Water Sinks'. For many years, it was believed that this river was the same as Malham Beck, which emerges further down the valley at the base of Malham Cove. However, dye tests have now proved that the water disappearing underground at Water Sinks does actually comes back to the surface much further downstream at Aire Head Springs between Hanlith and Malham village. The waters of Malham Beck mainly originate at another location on Malham Moor. It is clear that, despite the intrepid efforts of cave divers, an extensive network of cave systems lies waiting to be discovered in these limestone hills.

9. Turn left along a lane back to Kirkby Malham and the start.

Walk 15
MALHAM

This outstanding walk would surely figure in anybody's top ten Great English Walks – certainly it is near the top of the list for the author. The limestone scenery is breathtaking and the area has inspired poets and painters from Wordsworth and Turner onwards. This route visits all the fascinating geological features which make this corner of Yorkshire so interesting. The start I recommend is in Malham itself, close by the teashop (see notes about both possible starting points on next page)

 Malham is said to be the most popular destination in the Dales and so has many places to eat. Some of these tend towards being cafés rather than teashops. Beck Hall is in an idyllic position a couple of hundred yards from the centre of Malham and was originally a Dales yeoman's cottage that has grown over the centuries into a substantial building, now run as a guest house and tea rooms. Meals are served either in the dining room or the attractive large garden next to a stream, a few hundred yards from where it emerges at the bottom of mighty Malham Cove. The tearoom is open between noon and 5 pm every day in the summer and at weekends in winter and there is always a good selection of cakes and scones for tea. Telephone: 01729 830729. Website: www.beckhallmalham.com

DISTANCE: 5 miles plus an optional 1 mile extension to Gordale Scar.

MAP: OL2 Yorkshire Dales Southern & Western areas.

STARTING POINT: The National Trust informal car park south of Malham Tarn (GR 894657).

HOW TO GET THERE: From the A65 outside Settle take the B6479 Horton-in-Ribblesdale road. Turn right at Langcliffe, following the signs to Malham. At a sharp right-hand bend, continue in the same direction on a minor road, soon passing a National Trust sign saying 'Malham Park Estates'. Follow this for about 1½ mile to a car park on the left. Alternatively, Malham Tarn is signposted from Malham.

ALTERNATIVE STARTING POINT: I really enjoy my tea part way round a route so I can work up a good appetite and then walk off the effects of indulging it. The circuit described fits that pattern but the consequence of this here is that the return leg is not the gentle stroll I favour but involves almost all the climbing – two stiff pulls. The alternative start at Malham, where there is a large car park (charge) at the National Park information centre on the edge of the village, therefore has much to recommend it. From the car park turn left into Malham to pick up the route at point 7.

THE WALK

Before starting, walk away from the road a few yards to look over Malham Tarn. It is the highest stretch of water in the Pennines and is very shallow with a maximum depth of about 14 feet. During the Ice Age the porous limestone was eroded away exposing less permeable rock. Thus the lake was formed but it was much larger at that time. Being so shallow it easily fills up with material washed into it and the and this forms first bog and eventually dry land. The area is of considerable scientific importance and the building across the lake, Tarn House, is a field studies centre.

1. Cross the road and take a footpath signed 'Malham Raikes 1½ML'. Follow the path across the hillside, over a stile and on past paths on the right and left and some tiny tarns to the brow of the hill. Continue on the clear path as it starts to descend and magnificent views open up. When the path forks immediately after the third ladder stile, take the right fork to a wall corner.

2. At a wall corner follow the path to the left, walking with a wall on the right.

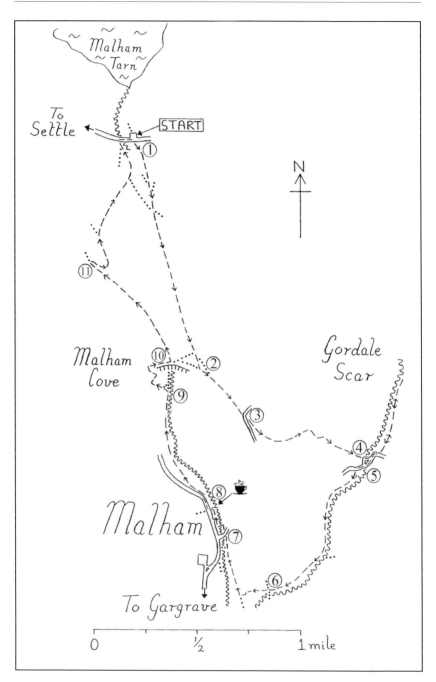

Malham Tarn

To Settle

START

①

N

⑪

Gordale Scar

Malham Cove

⑩ ② ③ ④ ⑤

⑨

⑧

Malham

⑦

⑥

To Gargrave

0   ½   1 mile

When this ends, continue on the path to a lane, passing either side of a small mound.

3. Cross the lane to a footpath 10 yards to the right, signed 'Gordale ¾M'. Follow the very clear path to another lane.

In the last field before this lane are the remains of a small Iron Age, Romano-British settlement dating back to between 300 BC and AD 400. Once you know they are there, you can see the outline of a number of hut circles together with signs of enclosure that were probably garden plots.

4. To visit Gordale Scar, turn left along the lane for about 80 yards and then take a path on the left into the scar. After wondering at the drama of the scene, retrace your steps.

Gordale Scar is one of the outstanding sights of the Dales and this extension is strongly recommended. The deep, narrow chasm was formed by the torrential melt water from the glaciers of the last Ice Age eating away at a pre-existing fault in the rock. It now has quite a small stream, which may disappear altogether in the driest weather, and such a spectacular gorge could not have been formed by the small beck we see today.

To continue the main walk, Turn right along the lane for 120 yards (straight on if you have been to Gordale Scar).

5. Take a path on the left, signed 'Malham 1½ML'. This soon forks – the left branch leads to the top of Janet's Foss and the right is the main riverside path. Follow the path downstream through a wooded gorge and then through flower filled meadows.

Janet's Foss is not a high waterfall but must rank among the most attractive in the National Park. The name 'Janet' is a corruption of 'Jenet', the Queen of the Fairies, who was reputed to live in a cave behind the cascade; 'foss' derives from force, a Yorkshire word for a waterfall. The cave is formed by an apron of tufa, pure calcium carbonate deposited from the water. Rainwater is naturally slightly acid and when it percolates through limestone it slowly dissolves the calcium carbonate of which the rock is formed. When it reaches the surface at a spring, chemical changes on contact with the air (and by the action of algae) cause the calcium carbonate to come out of solution and be redeposited as tufa. Much the same process forms stalagmites and stalactites in caves. The woods around the fall are ancient, which means they are known to have existed continuously from before

1600 . They form a rich profusion of trees and ground vegetation dominated by dog's mercury and wild garlic, which both like shady conditions.

6. At a junction where there is a walled lane on the right and a footbridge on the left, continue in the same direction through a kissing-gate, as indicated by arrows on a gatepost. Turn right at a T-junction with the Pennine Way and follow the clear path into Malham.

There has been a settlement at Malham at least from the Bronze Age and at different periods a living has been won in many ways. Before the Dissolution much of the land round the village was controlled by Fountains Abbey and Bolton Priory and sheep farming was important, as it remains today. Malham has also been a centre for lead and copper mining and once had a cotton mill. Today, the dominant industry is tourism with people drawn by the grandeur of the village's setting. You will see many attractive 18th and 19th-century buildings around the sloping green and the river is spanned by packhorse and clapper bridges but you may notice something is missing! That is a church. This is surprising in a village of such antiquity with strong ecclesiastical connections but in fact the church for all this part of the dale is a few miles down the road at Kirkby Malham, which literally means 'the church near Malham'.

7. Do not cross the river at the road bridge. Cross the road and continue by the river for 50 yards to a footbridge. Cross this and then turn right on a footpath on the opposite bank and continue upstream through the woods to emerge on a road. Turn right and then almost immediately turn right again on a track and over a clapper bridge to Beck Hall, built on the site of a building once owned by Fountains Abbey.

8. From the teashop return over the bridge and turn right along the lane. Just after the last building on the right take a path on the right, signed 'Malham Cove ½ml Malham Tarn 1¾ml', and follow the path towards the Cove.

Malham Cove is unique and breathtaking. It lies on the Middle Craven Fault, a crack or fault in the Earth's crust. The softer rocks to the south have dropped and been eroded leaving the escarpment as a prominent feature of the landscape. The actual line of the fault is just a little to the south of the cove as the rocks have been eroded back over the centuries. The exact geological processes which formed the Cove have been the subject of much speculation but it must have been some unusual combination of ice, water and earth movements. The novelist Charles Kingsley was a frequent visitor to Tarn House and included the Cove in 'The Water Babies'. Tom, the young chimney sweep, escapes from his cruel master by scrambling down the rock face.

9. Before reaching the base of the Cove, turn left to climb a well constructed series of steps, built to combat the erosion of visitors' feet. At the top cross a stile and follow the path onto the limestone pavement. Pick your way over this along the top of the Cove as far as a wall.

The strange, fissured stone is known as limestone pavement and was created by the action of ice and water on the rock. During the last Ice Age, some 15,000 years ago, massive glaciers covered the area and scoured the rock bare. When the ice retreated, the rock was exposed to rain. Limestone is slightly soluble in water and so the rain has slowly eaten into the rock, developing cracks and joints into large rounded rifts. These are called grykes and the slabs between are known as clints. If you examine the clints you will see that this process is still continuing as many have deep runnels worn by rainwater draining towards a gryke. The environment within the grykes is different from that on the surrounding rocks, being more shady, damper and cooler in summer and protected from the wind. This means a different community of plants can thrive in this protected situation, including many moisture loving ferns.

10. Do not cross the wall but turn left to walk with it on your right and follow the path as the valley gradually narrows to a dramatic gorge. At the end continue on the path up steps to climb out of the valley.

This dry valley, called Watlowes, was formed by melt water from glaciers flowing over still frozen ground. It must have formed a spectacular waterfall as it fell over Malham Cove. No water has been known to drop over the Cove since the early years of the 19th century.

11. Cross the stile at the top of the steps then turn sharp right on a path signed 'Malham Tarn 1'. Ignore a path leading left and continue by a wall on the right to a gate onto a road very close to the start.

Just before the road, a stream by the wall disappears into the ground. As the ground thawed at the end of the Ice Age, it became more permeable and water percolates into the rock rather than flowing over the surface, leaving the dry valley the route has just followed. Some of the water which disappears here may appear at the bottom of the Cove as Malham Beck but studies have shown that most of the beck water originates about a mile to the west of the Tarn near an old lead mine.

Walk 16
SETTLE

Setting off from the bustling market town of Settle, this walk captures the exhilaration and splendour of the limestone dales. This is one of the more energetic walks in this book, starting with a steady climb up the hill behind the town, but the effort is well rewarded by dramatic limestone scenery and stupendous views across Ribblesdale to the Forest of Bowland and even as far as the Lake District on a clear day. The route drops down to an old cotton mill just outside Settle on the river Ribble which today houses a visitor centre, after which it is an easy stroll back to the start.

 Watershed Mill, built as a cotton mill in 1849, was originally called Shed Mill. The building was used as an agricultural feed store in the 1950s and restored and opened as a business and craft centre in the 1990s. It houses some interesting shops and at the far end of the mill shop is Hector's coffee shop. This is named after Hector Christie who was the vice-chairman of the Fine Cotton and Doublers Association, a combine to which this mill belonged in the early years of the century. A light and airy place serving cakes, sandwiches and soup as well as full meals, it is open every day throughout the year from 10 am (11 am on Sunday) to 4.30 pm. Telephone: 01729 825539. Website www.watershedmill.co.uk

DISTANCE: 5 miles.

MAP: OL2 Yorkshire Dales Southern & Western areas.

STARTING POINT: Whitefriars car park, Settle (charge), 100 yards north of Market Place (GR 819638). Should this be full, there are two other signed car parks in Settle.

HOW TO GET THERE: Settle is on the B6480 and signed from the A65 which now, thankfully, bypasses the town.

ALTERNATIVE STARTING POINT: If you want to visit the teashop at the beginning or end of your walk, start at Watershed Mill, just outside Settle on the B6479 to Stainforth. The teashop is in the mill and there is a large car park. You will then start the walk at point 12.

THE WALK

1. Leave the car park and turn right to Market Place. Leave the square at the top left-hand corner up a steep lane called Constitution Hill.

Settle has been an important market town for centuries, having received its charter from Henry III in 1248. The market is still held on a Tuesday. If you have time, it is well worth wandering around the town as it has many interesting and attractive buildings, mainly Georgian but some earlier. Note especially the unusual Shambles at the top of the market which started life as a row of butchers' shops. The Folly, on the road towards Upper Settle, is so called because of its extravagant design and because Thomas Preston who built it in 1679 ran out of money.

2. At the top of the hill take a walled track uphill on the right. When the wall on the right ends, continue with the wall on the left for one field.

3. Turn right on a path signed 'Malham 5'. The path climbs beside a stone wall on the right until a path joins on the right. Continue on the path as the wall veers away to the right to reach a wall corner. Continue in the same direction, walking with a wall on the left and climbing less steeply.

Two notable features can be seen from this path. The green dome is part of the buildings of Giggleswick School, founded in 1507. The green colour comes from

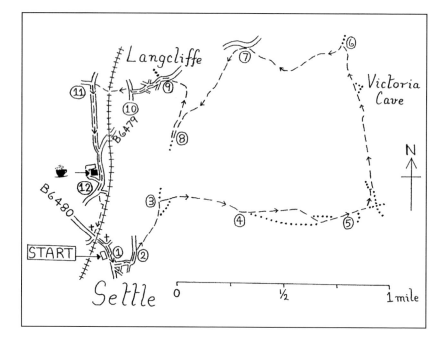

oxidation of the copper with which the dome is covered. Less attractive is the gash of Giggleswick Quarry, one of eight active quarries in the National Park (see also walk 18).

4. Go through a small gate by a field gate. After a further 90 yards the path forks. It doesn't matter which fork you take as they join up again a little farther on and both seem to be equally used; the one on the left is the public right of way. After the two branches rejoin at a gap in a wall, continue ahead with a wall on the right.

The striking scenery around Settle results from the dramatic limestone cliffs or scars thrown up by earth movements. Limestone is a relatively soft rock and has been shattered and weathered into dramatic shapes. The cliff ahead is called Attermire Scar. The name may derive from 'Outer Mere', suggesting that boggy land at its foot may once have been a tarn. Shallow ponds and lakes are, in geological timescales, temporary features in the landscape, soon filling in with sediment and becoming bog and then dry land.

5. After crossing a ladder stile over a wall, note a path over a ladder stile on the right signed 'Highside Lane 1ML'. Do not take this path but continue ahead for a further 120 yards then turn left on a faint, unsigned path. This climbs up through the rocks to a ladder stile over the wall on the right. Over the stile, turn left to continue uphill. At the top continue on the clear path along the bottom of the scar, passing below Victoria Cave to eventually arrive at a T-junction with a crosstrack.

Victoria Cave was discovered (or I should say rediscovered) in 1838 by a local man, Michael Horner, who was puzzled when his companion's dog disappeared into the hillside only to reappear a few yards further on. Horner's employer, a keen archaeologist and local tradesman called Joseph Jackson, led the excavations and the cave has proved a treasure house of pre-history. Buried in the clay on the floor of the cave were remains of animals such as bison, elephants, bears and rhinoceroses, who roamed this area in times past, together with relics of Stone Age people dating back to 10,000 BC. The cave was also inhabited by later groups, including use as a hiding place by Celts during the Roman occupation. Jewellery, pottery and tools have been found, some of which are in the British Museum and others can be seen in the Museum of North Craven Life in Settle. Jackson named the cave Victoria in honour of the young queen's coronation. Since then, the entrance has been enlarged. It consists of three large, damp and muddy chambers and nowadays there are notices warning of the dangers of exploration.

6. Turn left and walk along the track to a T-junction with a road.

7. Turn left through a gate on a bridleway, signed 'Settle 2'. Follow the path along the hillside, passing through three small gates.

8. After the third gate watch for a ladder stile over the wall on the right. Over this, walk back across the field to a gate to the right of a wood. As you will see, this is a laborious way of moving a few yards downhill to a path along the top of the wood but it is necessary if you are keen to stick to public rights of way. Follow the path down to the road on the edge of the village of Langcliffe.

9. Turn left through Langcliffe. This sometimes offers an alternative possibility for refreshment as teas are served at Langcliffe Institute on some Sundays in the summer. Continue through the village to a main road.

It is difficult to imagine that this peaceful place was once the scene of bloodshed and violence but in the 14th century the Dales suffered the attentions of Scottish raiders. In 1318 Langcliffe was completely destroyed and then rebuilt ½ mile south-east of its original site in a more defensible position. It is centred round a large green where cattle were guarded. This used to be graced by a huge sycamore which has recently been replaced by a young tree to grow into a worthy successor. Between 1912 and 1919 and again from 1921 to 1941 Langcliffe had a hot line to the world's news stories. Geoffrey Dawson, editor of The Times during these years, spent much of his time with his aunt at Langcliffe Hall. She would not have a telephone in the house so Dawson kept in touch with his office by messages relayed from the railway station in Settle. An earlier Dawson, Major William, was a close friend of Isaac Newton who often visited. Two gnarled apple trees in the garden of Langcliffe Hall are said to have grown from cuttings from a tree planted by Major Dawson to commemorate Newton's work on gravity.

10. Turn right for 10 yards and then take a walled path on the left. Follow this over a railway to a lane.

☕ **11.** Turn left. At the main road continue in the same direction for about 250 yards to Watershed Mill and the teashop on the right.

12. After tea, continue along the main road for another 100 yards. Turn left on a path immediately after a road on the left called Barrel Sykes and follow this until it emerges on a main road. Turn left under the railway, back to the start.

The towering railway arches carry the Settle-Carlisle railway, a line that many railway historians say should never have been built! In the 1860s the Midland Railway Company was trying to expand its operations from London to the North and ran trains as far as Ingleton, a few miles from here. The track northwards from Ingleton belonged to a competing company, the London North Western Railway, and they would not allow London Midland's trains access to the track. The solution seemed to be a new line to Carlisle, a route that had already been rejected by engineers because of the difficult terrain. A bill was put before Parliament to build this line, perhaps as a bluff to persuade LNWR to be more co-operative. If it was a bluff, it was an expensive one because the bill was passed and Parliament insisted the line be built. The line cost £3.5 million compared with the planned £2 million and extracted a heavy toll in deaths due to accident and disease among the army of navvies assembled to carry out the work. In the church opposite the car park is a plaque to the memory of those who lost their lives, paid for by their fellow workmen and the company. The railway stands today as an heroic feat of Victorian engineering. Often threatened with closure, the line has been repeatedly saved by public protest and now is an important tourist attraction in its own right as well as carrying visitors into the Dales.

Walk 17
AUSTWICK AND CLAPHAM

This is a superb walk connecting two exceptionally attractive Dales villages. En route it visits the Norber Erratics, one of the outstanding geological features of the Dales, from where there are stunning views. The walk can be shortened and made less strenuous by missing out a visit to these strange boulders but the extra effort is amply rewarded and I do urge you to make it. After this geological excursion, the route drops down to the lovely village of Clapham and you can reward yourself with a good tea. The return follows an ancient path across fields and is very easy walking.

Beautifully situated in the centre of Clapham, the Old Manor House is a mullioned farmhouse built in 1640. It now houses The Reading Room Cafe (and bar) and bunkhouse accommodation for groups visiting this part of North Yorkshire. As well as the cosy interior, there are some tables outside.

They serve a tempting selection of cakes as well as other teatime treats, such as scones with jam and cream and toasted teacakes. For lunch there is a good choice of sandwiches and filled jacket potatoes, as well as meat and potato pie with mushy peas and gravy. The cafe is open every day except Tuesday between 10 am and 5 pm, serving meals until 4.30pm. Telephone: 015242 51144. Website: www.claphambunk.com

DISTANCE: 4 miles.

MAP: OL2 Yorkshire Dales Southern & Western areas.

STARTING POINT: Round the village green in Austwick, opposite the Game Cock, it is possible to leave a few cars without causing inconvenience (GR 767685). If this is full, there are several other spots, notably Townhead Lane (see point 1 below).

HOW TO GET THERE: Follow the signs for Austwick from the A65 and continue through the village on the Horton road to the village green.

ALTERNATIVE STARTING POINT: If you want to visit the teashop at the beginning or end of your walk, start in Clapham where there is ample parking in the National Park car park. The teashop is by the entrance to the car park. You will then start the walk at point 7.

THE WALK

Austwick is a remarkably long, thin village and historians suggest that this is an indication that it started as a Norse community. Its name means Aust Wick or eastern settlement. There was a market here once but it moved on to neighbouring Clapham, leaving an attractive village with examples of domestic architecture from the 17th century to the present.

1. With your back to the Game Cock and facing the green, turn left through the village. Turn left up Townhead Lane and walk along this quiet byway out of Austwick as far as a walled crosstrack.

2. Turn left, signed 'Clapham 1½ Norber ½'. After 50 yards cross a stile on the right and follow a track across a field. At a gate leave the track to walk with a wall on the left to a small gate and stile then continue uphill by the wall. Follow the wall as it bends left.

(Note: to shorten the walk and miss out the visit to the Norber Erratics, continue along the walled track to rejoin the route at point 5.)

3. Some 50 yards after the wall bends left , at a large rock, look for a path joining on the right. Turn right along it, uphill and more or less back on yourself. At a signpost turn left uphill to reach an area dotted with huge grey

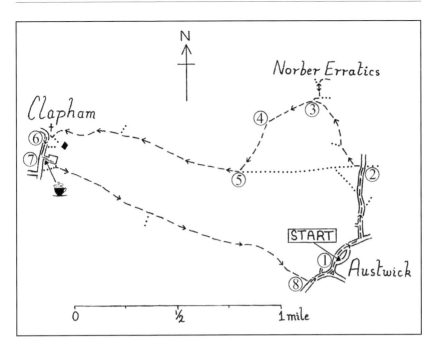

boulders. These are the Norber Erratics. The best ones lie over to the right.

The boulders appear unremarkable at first glance but closer inspection will reveal that many are perched on pedestals of limestone about a foot high. The rocks are much darker than the limestone beneath and are composed of Silurian gritstone formed about 100 million years earlier than the limestone on which they stand. They were carried by the glacier that once filled Crummack Dale and dropped in their present position as the ice melted about 12,000 years ago. The gritstone is much more resistant to erosion by rain, wind and frost than the softer limestone and has protected the rock beneath so the plinths could form; their height shows how much limestone has eroded away since the boulders were deposited at the end of the Ice Age. Such stray rocks, deposited by ice on top of stone formed in a different way and at a different time, are known as erratics. They are found wherever glaciers have passed but this is one of the best collections.

After inspecting this phenomenon, return past the signpost to the path by the wall. Continue along the path, walking with the wall on the left and crossing a ladder stile.

4. When the wall curves sharp left, head half left, skirting to the left of an

Norber Erratics

enclosed boggy area and to the right of a small area of limestone pavement to a ladder stile by a gate which gives onto a track known as Thwaite Lane, once part of the packhorse route between Richmond and Lancaster.

5. Turn right and follow the track to a lane by a church, passing through two tunnels.

The Farrer family has been influential in Clapham since the 18th century. Richard Farrer from Chipping in Lancashire settled in the village in 1716. One son, Oliver, became a solicitor in London and amassed a fortune through moneylending and plain living. It is said that he was known as Penny Bun Farrer because his meals often consisted of a penny bun and pump water. Another son, Thomas, made a fortune in India. Both brothers were childless and sent their wealth back to Clapham, enabling the family to buy Ingleborough Hall. The Farrers had a passion for landscaping and planting trees. In 1820 they dammed Clapham Beck to create an artificial lake and waterfalls. The most famous member of the family was Reginald (1880-1920), a well known botanist, who carried out much planting around the lake. He made many expeditions to the Far East, returning with new species of rhododendrons and other plants. The tunnels were constructed so the family could have easy access to the woods and lake without being bothered by travellers on Thwaite Lane. Today the woods and lake are open to the public on payment of a small charge and a trail leads to Ingleborough Cave. In 1837 a wall of stalagmites was broken down revealing a magnificent cave system beyond and this too is open to the public.

6. Turn left and follow the lane down into Clapham. The teashop is on the left, past the entrance to the National Park car park.

Clapham is clustered on both sides of Clapham Beck, spanned by four bridges, and was originally an Anglian settlement dating from about the 9th century. For the last 200 years or so it has been the estate village of the Farrers who once owned the entire village; even today the estate owns more than half the houses. As well as being widely regarded as one of the most attractive Dales villages and home of Reginald Farrer, Clapham has other claims to fame. Michael Faraday was one of the greatest experimental scientists this country has produced. He was born in London in 1791 but his father, James, was a blacksmith in Clapham before moving to London shortly after his marriage in 1786. Though Michael Faraday lived in London all his life, he was a Yorkshireman by descent and often referred proudly to his Yorkshire ancestry. In 1939 a monthly magazine, 'The Yorkshire Dalesman' was launched in Clapham. It has become one of the most successful publications of its type, today called simply 'The Dalesman'.

7. Take a path through the car park signed 'Austwick'. At the end of the car park turn right into a farmyard and turn left. Cross the farmyard to find a fenced path beside the yard then continue across fields. The path is easy to follow from stile to stile.

In the last field before the lane, note the terraces. These were laid out in medieval times for growing arable crops on land ploughed by ox teams. The stone walls, such an integral part of the landscape that it is difficult to imagine it without them, were built much later, in this case when Austwick Commons were enclosed in 1814.

8. At a lane on the outskirts of Austwick turn left and walk through the village, back to the start.

Walk 18
GARGRAVE

This walk lies outside the National Park but that doesn't stop it being a real gem and highly recommended. It uses two famous routes – the towpath of the Leeds Liverpool canal and the Pennine Way. The first part of the walk is beside the famous canal and is easy, level walking along a particularly attractive stretch. The route then crosses to the Pennine Way and the views from this path are superb. The Pennine Way leads into Gargrave and an interesting teashop, before a short stroll back to the start.

Even without the tasty and substantial food, the Dalesman in Gargrave is an interesting place to visit. In front of the tearoom is a genuine, old-fashioned sweet shop with all the old favourites in jars. They have over 50 different sweets including sugar mice, Pontefract cakes and walnut whips.

The tearoom itself is decorated with a fascinating collection of household memorabilia complemented by appropriate background music. A real nostalgia fest for those of a certain age! Behind the tearoom is a small shop specialising in antique gardenalia. The food is good Yorkshire fare – tasty, filling and reasonably priced – and I am not surprised it is particularly popular with cyclists. There is a good choice of cakes including fruitcake served the local way with cheese. As they point out, fruitcake without cheese is like a hug without a squeeze! For lunch there is a choice of sandwiches as well as things on toast and a choice of daily specials from the blackboard. The Dalesman is open every day except Monday throughout the year until 4.30 pm. Telephone: 01756 749250.

DISTANCE: 3 miles.
MAP: OS Explorer 10 Yorkshire Dales South
STARTING POINT: West Street car park, Gargrave. GR 932543
HOW TO GET THERE: From the A65, Settle to Skipton road, in Gargrave turn north along West Street next to the Dalesman to the car park on the right, opposite the Village Hall.
ALTERNATIVE STARTING POINT: This walk, unusually, starts close to the teashop as there is almost no parking elsewhere on the route. If you are keen to visit the teashop part way round the route there is a little parking, which can be very busy in summer, by the canal. To find this turn south towards the station in Gargrave and take the first road on the right. Follow this out of the village and round a sharp left-hand bend to a stretch by the canal where there is room for a couple of cars. You will then start the walk at point 4.

THE WALK
1. Facing the road go to the pedestrian access to the right. Turn right and immediately right again along West Street, signed 'Leeds Liverpool canal', and walk up to the canal.

The idea of the Leeds Liverpool canal was conceived in the middle of the 18th century to carry coal, wool, limestone and other goods across the north of England. Work started at both ends but there were endless delays and it did not open fully until 1816, having taken 46 years to build at a cost of five times the original budget. However, it must be considered a success as, unlike many canals, it competed successfully with railways and its commercial use continued into the second half of the 20th century. The canal reached Gargrave from Skipton in 1774 and gave a big boost to the economy of the area.

2. Immediately before crossing a bridge over the canal, turn left to walk with

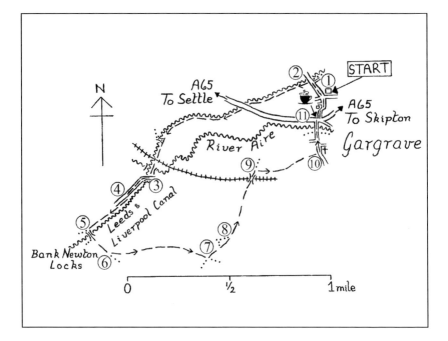

the canal on your right for a mile, until the path is forced up to a lane immediately after bridge 168.

The towpath passes under the A65 and the railway, transport links that have superseded the canal. It then dramatically crosses the Priest Holme Aqueduct over the river Aire (see walk 14).

3. Turn left along the lane to continue walking beside the canal, now on your left, for about 200 yards.

4. At a small lay-by go through a gate on to the towpath and carry on in the same direction, parallel with the road, to the next bridge, just after the second in a series of locks.

Though the canal reached Gargrave in 1774, note the date on the lock keeper's cottage, showing how long it took to continue westwards. This area was once an important base for canal maintenance with carpenter's workshops and other buildings that are now converted into houses. Not only that, one of the perks of working for the company was that employees were provided with a coffin on their death, and it was here that the coffins were made.

View from Priest Holme Aqueduct

5. Turn left over the bridge and go ahead to a field gate. Follow the track uphill.

6. At the top of the hill go through a gate. Now leave the track and bear half left across a field then walk with a fence on the left to a gate. Through the gate, keep ahead uphill, leaving the fence, to a second gate. Press on ahead, still climbing gently and enjoying the lovely views to the left, to an isolated finger post and clear cross track-like path.

7. Turn left along the Pennine Way. When the track turns left down towards a gate, continue in the same direction to find a stile by a gate in the far right corner of the field.

8. Over the stile turn right along the track and continue over a railway line.

9. Some 25 yards after the end of the railway bridge turn right up some steps and through a gate to carry on along the Pennine Way across the first field, half left across a second field, then along the right-hand side of a third field to a stile on to a drive. Turn right to soon reach a road in Gargrave.

Gargrave has a long history and is mentioned in the Domesday Book. Long before that there was a Roman villa just south of the present town (see notice board to right at the junction with the A65). Nothing can now be seen and the stones were taken to be reused, notably in the church. The present church dates mainly from the 19th century though the tower is older. Near the church was a moated manor and the moat can still be seen after wet weather from the path as you walk towards the church. Ian Macleod is buried in the churchyard. He was the son of a local doctor and was a rising politician in the 1960's who died suddenly less than a month after being made Chancellor of the Exchequer in 1970. Before entering politics he made his living as a professional bridge player and is best remembered among devotees of the game, of whom I am one, as one of the originators of Acol, the bidding system most widely played in Britain.

☕ **10.** Turn left, passing the church, to the main road and the teashop across the road.

Gargrave was the local market town but the coming of the canal encouraged the establishment of cotton mills in the 18th and 19th centuries and the industry thrived until 1932. When Airebank Mill closed, Gargrave fell into a depression until Johnson & Johnson took over the building in 1934, attracted by workers who could undertake the fine weaving that was needed to produce bandages. They are still here today as Systagenix, who export wound dressings all over the world.

11. Turn left out of the teashop and immediately left again along West Street back to the start.

Walk 19
DENT

*D*ent is hidden among a maze of tiny lanes in the dale to which it gives its name and, like its larger neighbour Sedbergh, is in the Yorkshire Dales National Park though in the county of Cumbria. This short walk climbs partly up the valley side to enjoy superb views of this lovely dale, richer in trees than many others. The route then drops down to the distinctive village of Dent for tea before a gentle return by the river to the start.

 Stone Close on Main Street, Dent, is an exceptionally attractive traditional teashop in a building originally dating from the 17th century which was once two farm cottages. It has retained many features such as exposed beams, flagged floors and open ranges. They prize themselves on using local produce, and there is an excellent selection of cakes to be enjoyed and the teas include Farrer's Lakeland, especially strong and sustaining. For a light lunch there are sandwiches and panninis and some interesting variants on Welsh Rarebit. Daily specials, including a vegetarian option, are also available. They are open all year every day except Monday (open Bank Holidays) and Tuesday between 10 am and 5 pm. Telephone: 01539 625231. Website:www.stoneclose.co.uk

When the teashop is closed, an alternative source of refreshment is the Sun in Dent which serves food.

DISTANCE: 3 miles.
MAP: OL2 Yorkshire Dales Southern & Western areas.
STARTING POINT: Barth Bridge (GR 695879).
HOW TO GET THERE: From Sedbergh follow the signs to Dent. Some 4½ miles from Sedbergh, immediately before a bridge over a river, park on a very wide verge where there is room to safely leave several vehicles.
ALTERNATIVE STARTING POINT: If you want to visit the teashop at the beginning or end of your walk, start in Dent where there is ample parking in the village car park (charge). The teashop is a few yards left along the road. You will then begin the walk at point 7.

THE WALK

1. Facing the road, turn right and walk across the bridge and along the road for another 150 yards.

2. Take a footpath on the right, signed 'Gawthrop ½', and follow it along the left-hand side of a field to a stile where the path crosses the wall and continues in the same direction on the other side, climbing and passing a pretty waterfall. At two gates go through the one on the left onto a track and turn left to a lane.

3. Turn right for 50 yards to some seats placed to admire the view over Dentdale. Turn left on a tiny lane, signed 'Dent ¾'. Pass Gawthrop Hall then follow the concrete track to the right of the next building. (Ignore a tempting path on the left signed 'Dent' unless you want a short cut that misses the best views on the walk. This path rejoins the route at point 5.) Watch for a kissing gate off the track as the track bends left. Go through this to continue in the same direction. This part of the path can be difficult and muddy but has good views into the valley carved by the stream. Press on to soon find another gate into a field. Keep ahead up the right hand side of the field to a metal field gate.

4. Go through the gate and ahead for 30 yards then turn left towards a barn to a stile in a wall back into the field you were in before. (For a pretty picnic

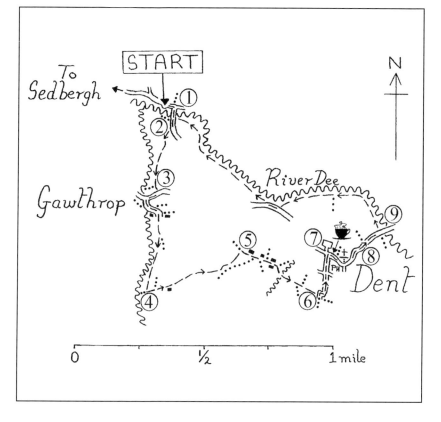

spot turn right to the river.) Cut across the corner of the field to a ladder stile then walk half left to a second ladder stile in the far left corner. Continue in the same direction to yet another ladder stile and then on to a step stile then walk down the right-hand side of a field to a gate. Through the gate, bear right down to join a track.

5. Turn right. Ignore a track on the left between barns and continue ahead between farm buildings to a metal field gate. Bear half right to a plank bridge over a stream and head across a field to a small gate. Do not be tempted to drift left down the hill or you will miss the stile and have to climb back up to it. Continue in the same direction, briefly joining a track, to a lane.

6. Turn left. Continue in the same direction at some crossroads to emerge on the main road opposite Dent car park. The teashop is a few yards to the right.

Dent is an exceptionally attractive village – or perhaps that should be town because, though its permanent population is now numbered in the hundreds, it has the feel of a bustling and important place. It is a beautiful cluster of whitewashed buildings and cobbled streets in a perfect setting among green hills. Dent's most famous son was Adam Sedgwick whose father was vicar here at the end of the 18th century. He was educated at Sedbergh school (see walk 20) and went on to become one of the founders of modern geology and a professor at Cambridge. He retained his connection with his home town and his distinguished career is honoured by a memorial, a slab of pink Shap granite, in the centre. Dent was also famous for its 'terrible knitters' – this did not mean they were incompetent, it was a compliment as they were terribly good and terribly fast This was an important cottage industry and the garments turned out were taken by horse and cart for sale in Kendal. The craft is maintained and locally produced items are for sale in The Shop on the Green.

7. Turn left as you leave the teashop and at Church Cottage continue ahead on a path to pass in front of the church to a lane.

St Andrew's has a Norman doorway though most of the church was rebuilt in the 19th century. It has some Jacobean pews and is floored with Dent marble. Both black and grey marble were quarried near here though the industry declined in the last century.

8. Turn left as far as a bridge.

9. Take a path on the left along the river bank, signed 'Hippens ½ML'. Follow this by the river, joining a road for about 100 yards before continuing on the riverside path to emerge on the road near the bridge at which the walk started.

Walk 20
SEDBERGH

The route described here is an idyllic short walk based on this ancient town which shelters an outstanding traditional teashop. The outward leg is on the side of the broad valley of the river Rawthey to the east of Sedbergh, along the base of the mass of Winder Fell towering over the town. The views are excellent, considering how little effort is involved in attaining them. After passing the site of a Norman castle, the route drops down into Sedbergh for tea. The return is an easy stroll on the bank of the river, attractively lined with many species of trees.

The Three Hares on Main Street in Sedbergh is a very interesting teashop. It shares its home with The Moocher, a company specialising in street food based round wild, foraged and rare breed ingredients and the snacks offered at lunchtime are different and delicious. For example, on my visit the menu featured chickpea fritters with raita, which was exceptionally

93

tasty, or goose confit risotto. The sandwiches are made with their own bread baked on the premises, as are the excellent scones and cakes. The Three Hares is open between 8.30 am (and serves breakfast if you are out and about early) and 5 pm every day throughout the year. Telephone: 015396 21058.

DISTANCE: 3½ miles.

MAP: OL19 Howgill Fells & Upper Eden Valley.

STARTING POINT: Straight Bridge over the river Rawthey on the A683 (GR 676923).

HOW TO GET THERE: Take the A683 Kirkby Stephen-Sedbergh road to the bridge, 1 mile east of Sedbergh, where there are two large laybys on the north side of the river.

ALTERNATIVE STARTING POINT: If you want to visit the teashop at the beginning or end of your walk, start in Sedbergh where there is ample parking in the town car park behind Main Street. The teashop is to the right along Main Street. You will then start the walk at point 9.

THE WALK

1. Facing the road, turn right for a few yards to the bridge then turn left on a public footpath, signed 'Buckbank ½ML'. Continue along the path as it bears away from the river and uphill in the second field. Follow it through a farmyard to a lane.

2. Turn right along the lane for 250 yards.

3. Just before a house on the left, turn left on a public footpath, signed 'Underbank 1m'. Follow the path along the right-hand side of a field to a stile. Over the stile, bear left, passing the end of a dry stone wall, and then head across a field bearing slightly left to a stile. Cross the next field to a further stile and then bear right to a farm.

4. Walk in front of Hollin Hill Farm. Do not go down the farm drive but continue in the same direction through a metal field gate and across a field to a footbridge over a stream. Walk along the right-hand side of a field to a large stone barn. Go through a field gate on the right on the far side of the barn then walk down the drive in front of a beautiful old stone house.

5. Some 40 yards after the drive to Ghyll Farm joins on the right, cross a stone stile by a small gate on the right then walk along the left-hand side of a field to a footbridge over a stream. Continue along the right-hand side of a field and then across a field to a stile by a gate.

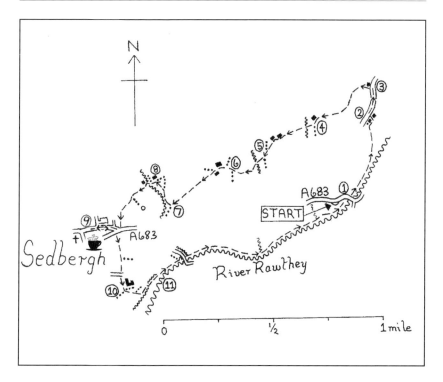

6. Turn right on a farm track and follow it between buildings. Stay on the main track, soon passing some houses on the left.

7. Just before the first house on the right, go through a metal kissing-gate on the right and follow the track up by a stream. As the track levels out, bear left, following a clear path, soon crossing three stiles and coming to a converted barn.

The prominent green mound seen through the trees to the left, and passed more closely a little further on, is Castle Haw. This is the site of a Norman motte-and-bailey castle which once guarded the Rawthey and Lune valleys against marauding Scots. The earth mound, or motte, on which the castle keep stood is 30 feet high and it was surrounded by an extensive courtyard or bailey. The castle, as was often the case, was probably built of wood as no signs of stonework have survived.

8. Turn left in front of the barn and bear left by a house. Follow this track down into Sedbergh. Turn right along Main Street, not the A683. The teashop is on the left.

Historic Sedbergh used to be the most westerly town in Yorkshire. Administrative fiat removed it to the composite county of Cumbria but it is still proud to be part of the Yorkshire Dales and is within the National Park. It grew up near the confluence of several rivers – the Rawthey, the Clough, the Dee and the Lune – and so at the junction of important valley trading routes. The town has held a market charter since 1251 and is still important in this way to the surrounding countryside. Built of local stone, the old centre has an intriguing maze of alleys behind the main street. Down one, Weavers Yard, is an old house with a huge chimney in which sheltered Bonnie Prince Charlie after the failure of the 1745 rebellion. Since 2006 Sedbergh has been developing as England's book town, similar to Hay-on-Wye in Wales and Wigtown in Scotland. This means there are numerous bookshops and other businesses involved in the book trade. If you enjoy poking around second-hand bookshops you will find it hard to drag yourself away.

9. Return along Main Street to the main road, where you joined it earlier. Cross the A683 and take the path opposite, signed 'Settlebeck or Millthrop'. When the track bends left, continue ahead through a kissing-gate next to a field gate. Cross a drive at the top of the hill and continue in the same direction by the wall of Winder House.

Sedbergh's most illustrious son is Roger Lupton, born nearby, who went on to become Provost of Eton and a canon of Windsor. He founded a chantry school in the town in 1525, endowing it with scholarships and fellowships at St John's College, Cambridge. It later became a free grammar school and then a public school. One of its earlier buildings, erected in 1716 and now a museum and library, is at the far end of the main street. The school is now housed in Victorian buildings to the south of the town. It has had several famous pupils. Adam Sedgwick, one of the fathers of modern geology, was born in nearby Dent and educated here (see walk 19). Coleridge's son, Hartley, was a master until he was sacked after a violent drinking bout.

10. When the wall ends, bear half left downhill, through two small gates and walk by a stream to reach the river bank at a weir.

11. Walk upstream by the river, bearing left at the first bridge to cross the road. Continue by the river to the next bridge and the start.